MOVIE NIGHT TRIVIA

Robb Pearlman

TRUE OR FALSE QUESTIONS
BY SHANE M. CARLEY

CIDER MILL PRESS

BOOK PUBLISHERS

KENNEBUNKPORT, ME

MOVIE

CIDER MILL
PRESS

BOOK
PUBLISHERS

KENNEBUNKPORT, ME

NIGHT TRIVIA

Robb Pearlman

TRUE OR FALSE QUESTIONS
BY SHANE M. CARLEY

13-Digit ISBN: 978-1604336108
10-Digit ISBN: 1604336102

This book may be ordered by mail from the publisher. Please include $4.95 for postage and handling. Please support your local bookseller first!

Books published by Cider Mill Press Book Publishers are available at special discounts for bulk purchases in the United States by corporations, institutions, and other organizations. For more information, please contact the publisher.

Cider Mill Press Book Publishers
"Where good books are ready for press"
12 Spring Street
PO Box 454
Kennebunkport, Maine 04046

Visit us on the Web! www.cidermillpress.com

Design by Sara Corbett
Cover by Bashan Aquart

Image on page 9 used under official license from Shutterstock.com
All other images are courtesy of Photofest, Inc.

Printed in China
2 3 4 5 6 7 8 9 10

CONTENTS

INTRODUCTION

When I think about movies, it's impossible not to think about the social aspect of going to see one. There's no doubt that film brings people together and creates conversation. I dare you to think about your favorite films of all time and not remember who was with you when you saw them. Or who you've wanted to share them with over the years.

A love for movies is absolutely responsible for bringing together the best group of friends I could possibly imagine. When we met at a Halloween party, we were dressed like Marilyn Monroe, Optimus Prime, Wednesday Addams, and various other movie characters. Over the years, we've been everything from Ghostbusters to Dr. Emmett Brown to the entire cast of characters from *Kill Bill*. We seriously love movies. In fact, it was this passion for film that brought about our movie-related YouTube channel "How It Should Have Ended," which has grown from being a fun hobby into our actual jobs!

As a group that loves to get together and celebrate film, *Movie Night Trivia* is right up our alley! I love that this book creates a little competition for film fans, but I have no doubt that the iconic images and fun questions will do far more than that: they'll bring you and your friends or family together over your shared love of movies! I can't wait to enjoy all the nostalgia and movie debate this dynamic little book creates—so let's turn the page, and get started!

Tina Alexander
Co-Creator/Producer/Writer
"How It Should Have Ended"
www.howitshouldhaveended.com

HOW TO USE THIS BOOK

The only thing better than watching movies is talking about movies. And the only thing better than that is challenging your—or better yet, your friends'—knowledge about them! So get your snacks and get comfortable, because Movie Night Trivia is about to start!

This book is divided into six feature presentations: Musicals and Comedies, Animals and Family Films, Fantasy and Science Fiction, Superheroes and Action, Drama and Classics, and Animated. Each contains 25 questions to answer, and also includes bonus short questions about everyone's favorite actors, actresses, directors, and quotes, as well as a True-or-False Lightning Round. And as an end-credits bonus, you'll find three levels of additional True-or-False questions!

Once you've completed a section, use the following levels to score:

0-5 CORRECT ANSWERS: Valet Parker: You've been stationed beneath a theater marquee long enough to be vaguely aware that movies exist.

6-10 CORRECT ANSWERS: Ticket Taker: You've memorized the run times of each movie, and have heard people talking on their way into the theater to know if you can wait for the home video release.

11-15 ANSWERS: Popcorn Popper: You've heard enough coming out of the theaters to know when the explosions, laughs, and uncontrollable weeping will happen.

16-20 ANSWERS: Projectionist: You've seen every movie a hundred times and can work even the most obscure references into any casual conversation.

21-25 ANSWERS: Theater Manager: You're an expert in the cinematic arts who knows what to see, what to skip, and what's coming soon.

But don't worry if you'd prefer to skip around or not keep score. Because just like sitting in a movie theater, nobody will know what you're doing (unless you're on your phone—put that away!).

MUSICALS

and COMEDIES

Whether you're in the mood to watch a kick line
or a kick in the pants, these films are sure to
stimulate your jazz hands and funny bones!

NAME THE 2014 FILM THAT CAN TRACE ITS TITLE CHARACTER'S ORIGINS TO AN 1885 POEM.

► **Annie** started out as "Little Orphant Annie," a poem written by James Whitcomb Riley, originally titled "The Elf Child." The poem served as inspiration for a 1918 silent movie, which led to Harold Gray's comic strip, first seen in 1924. Annie went on to star in her own radio show in 1930, a 1977 Broadway musical (which has been revived several times), an Off-Broadway musical sequel (1993's "Annie Warbucks"), a 1999 television movie, and two feature films in 1982 and 2014.

WHICH PRINCESS APPEARS IN 2014'S **INTO THE WOODS**?

- A **SNOW WHITE**
- B **CINDERELLA**
- C **AURORA**
- D **ARIEL**
- E **BELLE**

► Though the princes allude to meeting Snow White and Aurora in the stage version of Stephen Sondheim's musical, **Cinderella** is the only princess to appear in the film adaptation.

IN 2012'S
LES MISERABLES,

JEAN VALJEAN WAS ORIGINALLY SENT TO JAIL FOR STEALING _____.

▶ *Les Misérables*, based on Victor Hugo's 1862 historical fiction novel takes place in pre-Revolutionary France. Times were tough back then. So tough, in fact, that Jean Valjean was forced to steal **a loaf of bread** to feed his starving family.

IN 2008'S
MAMMA MIA!,

DONNA, ROSIE, AND TANYA, BETTER KNOWN AS _____, REUNITE TO SING "SUPER TROUPER" AT SOPHIE'S BACHELORETTE PARTY.

▶ **Donna and the Dynamos**, an ABBA-singing trio played by Meryl Streep, Julie Walters, and Christine Baranski, are joined by their costars to sing "Dancing Queen" and "Waterloo" during the credits.

WHICH SONG IS NOT FROM 1965'S

THE SOUND OF MUSIC?

Ⓐ "DO-RE-MI"

Ⓑ "EDELWEISS"

Ⓒ "MY FAVORITE THINGS"

Ⓓ "PURE IMAGINATION"

Ⓔ "THE LONELY GOATHERD"

▶ **"Pure Imagination"** was written for 1971's *Willy Wonka and the Chocolate Factory* by Leslie Bricusse and Anthony Newley. The film, based on Roald Dahl's *Charlie and the Chocolate Factory*, was nominated for an Oscar for Best Original Score. *The Sound of Music* featured songs by the award-winning duo of Rodgers and Hammerstein.

WHICH 1980S JOHN HUGHES MOVIE DOES BECA RELUCTANTLY WATCH IN 2012'S

PITCH PERFECT?

A PRETTY IN PINK

B FERRIS BUELLER'S DAY OFF

C SIXTEEN CANDLES

D THE BREAKFAST CLUB

E SOME KIND OF WONDERFUL

▶ 1985's *The Breakfast Club*, whose closing credits song, "Don't You Forget About Me" by Simple Minds, becomes part of the Barden Bellas' winning routine.

IN 2003'S **ELF**, BUDDY VISITS HIS FATHER, WALTER, AT HIS OFFICE LOCATED IN _____, ONE OF THE WORLD'S MOST ICONIC BUILDINGS.

Remember.

▶ Though New York's **Empire State Building** is home to many businesses, no children's publishing companies currently operate out of its storied stories. It has, however, played crucial roles in such films as the 1933 and 2005 versions of *King Kong*, 1993's *Sleepless in Seattle*, and 1957's *An Affair to*

HITTING THEATERS BETWEEN 1998'S

STAR TREK INSURRECTION

AND

STAR TREK NEMESIS (2002), _____

IS OFTEN CALLED THE BEST "STAR TREK" MOVIE EVER MADE.

◀ An ode to fandom, pop culture conventions, and television space operas, 1999's *Galaxy Quest* features characters and situations that bear a striking similarity to the tropes first seen in the original "Star Trek" television series.

WHICH OF THE FOLLOWING CHARACTERS DOES NOT SUIT UP AS A GHOSTBUSTER IN THE 1984 FILM:

- **A** VENKMAN
- **B** STANTZ
- **C** SPENGLER
- **D** BARRETT
- **E** ZEDDMORE

▶ Ghostbusters Peter Venkman (Bill Murray), Ray Stantz (Dan Aykroyd), Egon Spengler (Harold Ramis) and Winston Zeddmore (Ernie Hudson) come to the aid of Dana **Barrett** (Sigourney Weaver), whose apartment building serves as a gateway for the evil Sumerian god, Gozer the Gozerian.

Wilson Phillips sang their 1990 hit song, "Hold On," in the wedding scene of 2011's Oscar-nominated comedy _____.

▶ **The band, composed of Carrie Wilson, Wendy Wilson, and Chynna Phillips, surprised a bride and her *Bridesmaids*, played by Maya Rudolph, Kristen Wiig, Melissa McCarthy, Ellie Kemper, Wendi McLendon-Covey, and Rose Byrne.**

NAME KIP DYNAMITE'S BRIDE IN 2004'S

NAPOLEON DYNAMITE

A LAFAWNDUH

B SHONDRELLA

C LATISCHA

D TIFFANY

E SUMMER

► Kip meets, gets makeover by, and marries **LaFawnduh**, his internet girlfriend, played by Shondrella Avery.

WHICH U.S. CITY IS THE SETTING FOR 2007'S **HAIRSPRAY**?

A BOSTON

B BALTIMORE

C CLEVELAND

D DETROIT

E BAYONNE

► Like many of John Waters' films, including 1972's Pink Flamingos, 1981's Polyester, and 1988's original non-musical version of Hairspray, Tracy Turnblad says (or in this case, sings) "Good Morning, **Baltimore!**"

REAL LIFE NEWSMAN BILL KURTIS PROVIDED NARRATION FOR 2004'S _____, A FILM ABOUT A TOTALLY MADE UP 1974 NEWSTEAM.

► Whether it's covering the news or rumbling till the cops come, San Diego's most popular *Anchorman*, Ron Burgundy (Will Ferrell), and his friends and colleagues Veronica Corningstone, "Champ" Kind, Brick Tamland, and Brian Fantana (Christina Applegate, David Koechner, Steve Carrell, and Paul Rudd) keep San Diego as classy as they can.

Name the teachers Cher plays matchmaker for in 1995's

CLUELESS.

BONUS QUESTION

Name the director who made silent appearances is most of his films, including *Spellbound* (1945), *North by Northwest* (1959), and *Psycho* (1960).

◄ Alfred Hitchcock.

◄ Based on Jane Austen's *Emma*, *Clueless*'s well-meaning main character, Cher, inserts herself into other peoples' lives, including **Ms. Geist**, played by Twink Kaplan and based on the novel's Miss Taylor, and **Mr. Hall**, played by Wallace Shawn, based on Mr. Weston.

IN 2004'S

SHAUN OF THE DEAD,

SHAUN (SIMON PEGG) AND ED (NICK FROST) TRY, UNSUCCESSFULLY, TO FIGHT OFF THE ZOMBIES THEY MEET IN THEIR BACKYARD BY _____.

▶ Despite their status as hipster collectibles, the roommates think they can stave off their doom by throwing vinyl records at the undead. It does not work.

BONUS QUESTION

Name the actor who played a human in *Planet of the Apes* in 1968 and an ape in *Planet of the Apes* in 2001.

▶ Charlton Heston

THOUGH IT'S HARD TO BELIEVE
THAT THERE WAS EVER A TIME WHEN
ALL PASSENGERS ON DOMESTIC FLIGHTS
WERE OFFERED MEALS, PASSENGERS
IN 1980'S **AIRPLANE!**
HAD A CHOICE OF CHICKEN OR FISH.
WHICH ONE MADE EVERYONE SICK?

► Surely you remember the **fish** sickened everyone aboard, including the pilot and co-pilot, played by Peter Graves and Kareem Abdul-Jabbar. And stop calling me Shirley.

WHAT COLOR IS
ANDY'S BLUE SWEATER
IN 2006'S

THE DEVIL
WEARS PRADA?

► It's not blue, it's not turquoise, and it's not lapis, it's cerulean.

Name the entertainer, known as Mr. Las Vegas, who makes a surprise cameo in the slide show at the end of 2009's

THE HANGOVER.

A Wayne Newton

B David Copperfield

C Elton John

D Frank Sinatra

E Barry Manilow

Wayne Newton, who rose to fame with his 1963 hit song "Danke Schoen," is so associated with Las Vegas that one of the streets servicing the city's airport is named Wayne Newton Boulevard.

SPELL

"supercalifragilisticexpialidocious."

▶ Robert and Richard Sherman, who wrote this and the other songs for 1964's Mary Poppins (and were played by B.J. Novak and Jason Schwartzman in 2014's Saving Mr. Banks), also wrote music for Walt Disney's "Carousel of Progress" and "Enchanted Tiki Room," theme park attractions as well as a host of other films for Disney and other companies.

THOUGH PEOPLE CAN TELL WHICH BATMAN IS WHICH, MANY THINK BILL PAXTON AND BILL PULLMAN ARE THE SAME PERSON. NAME THE BAT/BILL PAIR WHO STARRED IN 1992'S

NEWSIES.

A MICHAEL KEATON AND BILL PAXTON

B CHRISTIAN BALE AND BILL PULLMAN

C GEORGE CLOONEY AND BILL PAXTON

D VAL KILMER AND BILL PULLMAN

E BEN AFFLECK AND BILL PAXTON

◄ **Christian Bale** (Bruce Wayne/Batman in *Batman Begins, The Dark Knight,* and *The Dark Knight Rises*) and **Bill Pullman** (*Independence Day, Spaceballs*) starred in Disney's musical about an 1899 newsboy strike.

BONUS QUESTION

Name the actor who starred in the eponymous roles of *Cry-Baby* (1990), *Donnie Brasco* (1997) and *Rango* (2011).

◄ Johnny Depp

17

SOUTHERNER MELANIE HAS TO RETURN HOME TO FINALIZE HER DIVORCE FROM JAKE SO SHE CAN MARRY ANDREW, THE SON OF NEW YORK'S MAYOR, IN _____.

- (A) **SOMETHING TO TALK ABOUT**
- (B) **SWEET HOME ALABAMA**
- (C) **COUNTRY STRONG**
- (D) **THE NOTEBOOK**
- (E) **A WALK TO REMEMBER**

▶ Reese Witherspoon's Melanie has to travel back to *Sweet Home Alabama* to sort out her past with Josh Lucas's Jake before she can start her future with Patrick Dempsey's Andrew.

TO COUNTERACT THEIR ILLEGAL ACTIVITIES, THE CHARACTERS IN _____, A 2008 COMEDY, FIND THEMSELVES LARPING, WHICH IS COMPLETELY LEGAL.

▶ Happy endings abound for *Role Models'* Danny and Wheeler (Paul Rudd and Seann William Scott) as they LARP (Live Action Role Play) with their mentees Augie and Ronnie (Christopher Mintz-Plasse and Bobb'e J. Thompson).

IN NATIONAL LAMPOON'S VACATION,

THE GRISWOLDS SET OUT IN THEIR STATION WAGON TOWARD A FUN-FILLED TIME AT _____.

A ITCHY AND SCRATCHY LAND

B ZOMBIELAND

C SIX FLAGS

D WALLEY WORLD

E FUTURE WORLD

► The summer of 1983 found Clark, Ellen, Audrey, and Rusty Griswold (Chevy Chase, Beverly D'Angelo, Dana Barron, and Anthony Michael Hall) taking a "Holiday Road" trip to *Walley World*, but, finding it closed, take security guard Russ Lasky (John Candy) hostage instead.

DUE TO THE POPULARITY OF MILTON'S _____ IN 1999'S

OFFICE SPACE,

THE SWINGLINE COMPANY FINALLY STARTED MAKING THEM IN THE COLOR IN 2002.

BONUS QUESTION

Name the groundbreaking actor who played a prisoner who tried to break literal chains in *The Defiant Ones* (1958) and a doctor who broke societal ones in *Guess Who's Coming to Dinner* (1967).

◄ Sidney Poitier

► Thanks to the vocal fans of the home video version of Mike Judge's cult hit, the Swingline company began to produce red staplers three years after the movie premiered.

Name the 1991 film that was a remake of a 1950 movie of the same name, which starred Spencer Tracy, Joan Bennett, and Elizabeth Taylor.

► *Father of the Bride*, starring Steve Martin, Diane Keaton, and Kimberly Williams-Paisley. The trio also starred in the film's 1995 sequel, *Father of the Bride Part II*, itself a modern-take on the original film's sequel, 1995's *Father's Little Dividend*.

MUSICALS + COMEDIES

Q True or False: The infamous gopher from *Caddyshack* survives every attempt made by Carl Spackler (Bill Murray) to kill it.

Q True or False: In *The Naked Gun*, the baseball player programmed to assassinate the Queen of England was Dave Winfield of the Yankees.

Q True or False: In the film *Borat*, the woman Borat attempts to kidnap and marry is Pamela Anderson.

Q True or False: The older fraternity member who passes away in the film *Old School* goes by the nickname "Blue."

Q True or False: Nadia, Jim's love interest in *American Pie*, is a new student whose family just moved from a neighboring town.

Q True or False: The primary villain in *Blazing Saddles*, played by Harvey Korman, is named Marlon Monroe, causing many people to accidentally refer to him by the name of famous actress Marilyn Monroe.

Q True or False: Mel Brooks' *The History of the World, Part I*, set the stage for its Oscar-winning sequel, *The History of the World, Part II*.

Q True or False: *Monty Python and the Holy Grail* features characters including Sir Robin, Patsy, Tim the Enchanter, and Sir Not-Appearing-In-This-Film.

Q True or False: In the film *Happy Gilmore*, the title character's first love is not golf, but hockey.

A True. The movie concludes with the gopher emerging from the destroyed golf course and dancing to "I'm Alright" by Kenny Loggins.

A False. The Angels' Reggie Jackson was the sleeper cell activated during the game.

A True. Borat falls in love with her after seeing an episode of *Baywatch* for the first time.

A True. Actually named Joseph Pulasky, Blue was the oldest member of the new fraternity.

A False. Nadia is actually a foreign exchange student from Slovakia.

A False. Korman's character is named Hedley Lamarr, a name intentionally similar to that of actress Hedy Lamar.

A False. Despite its name (and a "coming attractions" gag at the end of the film), *The History of the World, Part I*, was a standalone film, and a sequel was never produced.

A True. Sir Not-Appearing-In-This-Film was used in a gag at the beginning of the movie, during the rundown of King Arthur's Knights of the Round Table.

A True. Later in the film, Chubbs (Carl Weathers) gives Happy (Adam Sandler) a putter shaped like a hockey stick.

MUSICALS + COMEDIES

Q True or False: At the beginning of every loop in *Groundhog Day*, the song that Phil Connors (Bill Murray) wakes up to is "I Got You Babe," by Sonny and Cher.

Q True or False: The protagonists in the film *Super Troopers* are state police officers in Maine.

Q True or False: In *Coming to America*, the final straw that causes Prince Akeem (Eddie Murray) to leave his home country of Zamunda is when his royal parents force him to take a job to earn his keep.

Q True or False: In *Dumb and Dumber*, Lloyd (Jim Carrey) pranks Harry (Jeff Daniels) with coffee spiked with sleeping pills, causing him to fall asleep at the wheel.

Q True or False: The first appearance of famous film duo Jay and Silent Bob was in the 1994 movie *Clerks*.

Q True or False: In *Who Framed Roger Rabbit*, Detective Eddie Valiant (Bob Hoskins) has a longstanding dislike for "Toons" because his brother was killed by one.

Q True or False: At 93 minutes, *Annie Hall* is the shortest film to ever win the Oscar for Best Picture.

Q True or False: In the bowling film *Kingpin*, Roy Munson (Woody Harrelson) loses a hand after a hustling scheme orchestrated by Ernie McCracken (Bill Murray) goes awry.

A True. Originally released in 1965, the song made a surprise charge up the charts when the 1993 film hit theaters.

A False. Although they do operate near the Canadian border, Troopers Ramathorn, Rabbit, Farva, and the rest are Vermont State Police officers.

A False. Tired of his life of luxury, Prince Akeem comes to America to avoid an arranged marriage thrust upon him by his parents.

A False. Lloyd actually spikes Harry's coffee with laxatives, leading to an entirely different (and equally embarrassing) situation.

A True. Though the characters would later take on a life of their own, Jay and Silent Bob made their initial appearance as a pair of slackers hanging out outside a convenience store.

A True. His brother was killed when a piano was dropped on his head by a Toon.

A False. *Annie Hall* is just barely edged out by the film *Marty*, which clocks in at 91 minutes.

A True. Munson features a prosthetic hand for the remainder of the film.

MUSICALS + COMEDIES

Q True or False: In Stanley Kubrick's dark comedy *Dr. Strangelove*, Peter Sellers plays three different characters, including the titular scientist.

Q True or False: In *The Big Lebowski*, the protagonists are obsessed with competing in their local softball league.

Q True or False: In *Brewster's Millions*, Montgomery Brewster's quest to spend $30 million and earn the rest of his inheritance leads him to personally finance a third party candidate in the New York City mayoral race.

Q True or False: The public figure that Derek Zoolander (Ben Stiller) is programmed to assassinate in *Zoolander* is the Prime Minister of Malaysia.

Q True or False: Miracle Max (Billy Crystal) brings Westley (Cary Elwes) back to life using a giant, chocolate-covered pill in 1988's *The Princess Bride*.

Q True or False: The famous line "I'll have what she's having" was first uttered in the classic romantic comedy *When Harry Met Sally*.

Q True or False: Football comedy *The Replacements* features Keanu Reeves as Jimmy McGinty, a washed-up coach drawn out of retirement to coach a team of replacement players during a strike.

Q True or False: While exploring the Los Angeles area, the protagonists in *Zombieland* are shocked to find Sylvester Stallone alive and well in his Beverly Hills mansion.

A True. Sellers plays President Muffley, Captain Mandrake, and the titular Dr. Strangelove.

A False. Bowling is the sport of choice for The Dude and his friends.

A False. Brewster does finance a campaign, but rather than back a specific candidate, his campaign urges people to vote for "none of the above."

A True. Thankfully, Zoolander is able to perfect his ultimate model look, "Magnum," in time to stun the crowd and save the Prime Minister's life.

A True. According to Max's wife, "the chocolate coating helps it go down easier."

A True. The line is widely considered to be one of the funniest in movie history.

A False. The role of McGinty is played by Gene Hackman, while Keanu Reeves plays Shane Falco, a formerly great college quarterback who was never given a fair shot in the pros.

A False. Instead of Stallone, the crew finds Bill Murray surviving with the help of some extremely convincing zombie makeup.

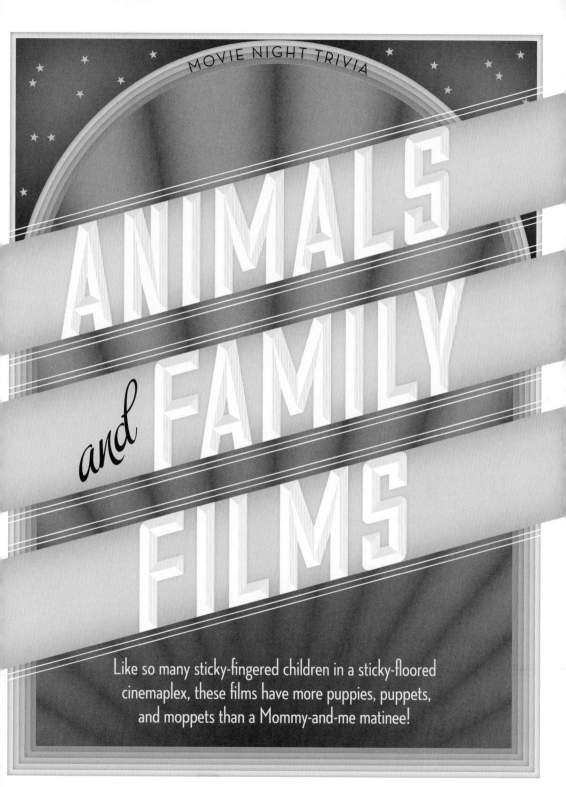

ANIMALS and FAMILY FILMS

Like so many sticky-fingered children in a sticky-floored cinemaplex, these films have more puppies, puppets, and moppets than a Mommy-and-me matinee!

2006'S NIGHT AT THE MUSEUM TAKES PLACE IN THIS ICONIC MUSEUM.

A THE SMITHSONIAN

B NATURAL HISTORY MUSEUM OF LOS ANGELES COUNTY

C THE AMERICAN MUSEUM OF NATURAL HISTORY

D THE METROPOLITAN MUSEUM OF ART

E THE HERMITAGE

BONUS QUESTION

Name the actor who wore a hook in *Hook* (1991) and a dress in *Tootsie* (1982).

▶ Each night, the exhibits of New York City's **American Museum of Natural History**, including dinosaurs, presidents, and Roman soldiers come to life for Ben Stiller's Larry Daley.

◀ Dustin Hoffman

IN AN EFFORT TO SAVE THEIR GOON DOCK COMMUNITY,

USE

AN ANTIQUE MAP TO TRY TO FIND ONE-EYED WILLIE'S TREASURE.

▶ A group of kids, dubbed *The Goonies*, race against time, and the evil Fratelli family, in the 1985 film of the same name.

Four Disney Princesses

(well, the actresses who provided their voices, at least) appeared in another Disney film featuring a different singing princess, 2007's

_____.

▶ Idina Menzel (Frozen's Elsa), Judy Kuhn (Pocahontas), Jodi Benson (The Little Mermaid's Ariel), and Paige O'Hara (Beauty and the Beast's Belle) were all enchanting in Enchanted.

JEFF KINNEY, UPON WHOSE 2007 BOOK THIS 2010 FILM WAS BASED, HAS OPENED HIS OWN BOOKSTORE IN MASSACHUSETTS.

◄ Jeff Kinney, author of the "Diary of a Wimpy Kid" books that were the basis for *Diary of a Wimpy Kid* (2010), *Diary of a Wimpy Kid: Rodrick Rules* (2011), and *Diary of a Wimpy Kid: Dog Days* (2012).

WHICH PHRASE IS USED BY FARMER HOGGETT IN 1995'S BABE?

A "THINK ON IT, PIG. THINK ON IT."

B "THAT'S ALL, PIG. THAT'S ALL."

C "THANK YOU, PIG. THANK YOU."

D "THAT'LL DO, PIG. THAT'LL DO."

E "BAAA-RAM-EWE, PIG. BAAA-RAM-EWE."

◄ Farmer Hoggett (played by James Cromwell) tenderly and modestly praises our porcine hero by saying, "That'll do, Pig. That'll do."

THE IMPORTANCE OF A BASEBALL FEATURING THE SIGNATURE OF _____ IS HOTLY DEBATED BY THE PLAYERS IN 1993'S **THE SANDLOT**.

► Nicknamed, among other things, "The Sultan of Swat," "The King of Crash," and "The Colossus of Clout," poor Smalls, played by Tom Guiry doesn't know that **Babe Ruth** is also "The Great Bambino."

WHETHER HE'S BEING BOUGHT OR SOLD, SAVING PEOPLE OR IN NEED OF SAVING HIMSELF, THE OPTIMISTIC EQUINE HERO OF THIS 1994 FILM NEVER HAS A LONG FACE.

► Based on an 1877 novel by Anna Sewell, and narrated by Alan Cumming, who serves as the voice of the title character, **Black Beauty** follows a horse from his birth through his tumultuous life to his happy retirement on Thoroughgood Farm.

Set on a farm, 1973's animated musical _____, based on a book by E.B. White, was produced by the company best known for creating cartoons set in the stone age, the future, and in Jellystone Park.

▶ Hanna-Barbera, who gave us "The Flintstones," "The Jetsons," and Yogi Bear, produced Charlotte's Web.

IN 2011'S **THE MUPPETS**, LIFELONG FAN GARY HOPES TO JOIN HIS FAVORITE TELEVISION TROUPE BY PERFORMING WHICH TALENT:

(A) DRUMMING

(B) SINGING WITH CHICKENS

(C) CHEMISTRY

(D) WHISTLING

(E) GOPHERING

▶ Though reluctant to show off his talents, Gary is most adept at **whistling**. Leave the drums to Animal, the chickens to Gonzo, chemistry to Professor Bunsen Honeydew and Beaker, and gophering to Scooter.

THIS 2011 FILM COULD HAVE BEEN CALLED "WINTER'S TAIL," BUT THAT MAY HAVE LEAD PEOPLE TO THINK THAT IT WAS A SHAKESPEAREAN ADAPTATION RATHER THAN A STORY ABOUT A DOLPHIN WHO IS OUTFITTED WITH A PROSTHETIC AFTER A MISHAP WITH A CRAB TRAP.

▶ Based on a true story, *Dolphin Tale* spawned a sequel in 2014. But don't worry, William Shakespeare, who wrote "A Winter's Tale" had a long and prolific career of his own.

IN THE CLIMACTIC SCENE OF 1993'S

FREE WILLY,

WHAT DOES WILLY JUMP OVER TO REACH FREEDOM?

A   **A SEAWALL**

B   **A DAM**

C   **A HIGHWAY**

D   **A WATERFALL**

E   **A BRIDGE**

▶ In a scene that could have ended much differently had he landed on Jesse (played by Jason James Richter), Willy, an orca (played by Keiko, also an orca), jumps over a seawall to get from a marina to the open water to meet his pod.

IN DISNEY'S 1961 CLASSIC
101 DALMATIANS,
PONGO AND PERDITA ADOPTED
THIS MANY PUPPIES:

- **A** 12
- **B** 99
- **C** 48
- **D** 51
- **E** 84

◄ Pongo + Perdita + 15 biological puppies+ 84 adopted puppies = 101 Dalmatians!

SOUNDER, BASED ON THE AWARD-WINNING BOOK, TELLS THE TALE OF A FARMING FAMILY AND THEIR DOG. UNLIKE THE BOOK, THE MAJORITY OF THE HUMAN CHARACTERS IN THE FILM HAVE _____.

◄ While the Great Depression denied Sounder's family their livelihood, author William H. Armstrong chose to also deny them **names**. The film, however, assigned names to Rebecca, Nathan Lee, and David Lee Morgan, the characters portrayed by Cicely Tyson, Paul Winfield, and Kevin Hooks.

IN 1989'S,
HONEY, I SHRUNK THE KIDS,
THE KIDS HAD TO TRAVERSE WHAT TREACHEROUS TERRAIN TO GET BACK HOME?

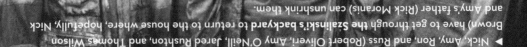

► Nick, Amy, Ron, and Russ (Robert Oliveri, Amy O'Neill, Jared Rushton, and Thomas Wilson Brown) have to get through the Szalinski's backyard to return to the house where, hopefully, Nick and Amy's father (Rick Moranis) can unshrink them.

IN **HOME ALONE,**

KEVIN MCALLISTER AMUSES AND EDUCATES HIMSELF BY WATCHING THIS BLACK AND WHITE GANGSTER FILM:

A ANGELS WITH FILTHY SOULS

B ANGELS WITH DIRTY FACES

C THE WILD ANGELS

D THE TROUBLE WITH ANGELS

E ANGELS IN THE OUTFIELD

BONUS QUESTION

Name the actor who transferred his role from Broadway to 1996's *A Funny Thing Happened on the Way to the Forum*, but did not do the same for the 1971 adaptation of *Fiddler on the Roof*.

◀ *Angels with Dirty Faces* (1938), *The Wild Angels* (1966), *The Trouble with Angels* (1966) and *Angels in the Outfield* (1994) are all real films, while "**Angels with Filthy Souls**" was created especially for the 1990 film starring Macaulay Culkin.

◀ Zero Mostel

In 2002's
TUCK EVERLASTING,

the Tuck family will never die because they _____.

BONUS QUESTION

Name the director who appeared in her director father's films including all three *Godfather* films (1972, 1974, 1990).

1950's

HARVEY

IS ABOUT

ELWOOD P. DOWD

AND HIS

BESTIE,

A _____.

▶ Elwood, played by Jimmy Stewart, has a deep and heartfelt friendship with Harvey, a giant invisible rabbit.

NAME THE 1993 SEQUEL TO 1989'S

LOOK WHO'S TALKING AND
1990'S **LOOK WHO'S TALKING TOO,**
IN WHICH AUDIENCES COULD HEAR
THE INNER VOICES OF ROCKS, A MUTT,
AND DAPHNE, A POODLE.

- Ⓐ LOOK WHO'S BARKING
- Ⓑ LOOK WHAT'S TALKING
- Ⓒ LOOK WHO'S STILL TALKING
- Ⓓ LOOK WHO'S TALKING NOW
- Ⓔ PLEASE STOP TALKING

► Danny DeVito and Diane Keaton joined the trilogy's returning stars John Travolta and Kirstie Alley to provide the speaking voices of the doggone stars of Look Who's Talking Now.

Starring Michael J. Fox, Hugh Laurie, Geena Davis, and Nathan Lane, the title character of this 1999 film is adopted into a family whose descriptive last name perfectly fits his diminutive stature.

◄ Based on a novel by E.B. White, *Stuart Little* is a little mouse with a big heart.

In 1992, the cacophonous movements of a Saint Bernard named _____ brought a lot of mischief, slobber, and love into a classic family led by Charles Grodin and Bonnie Hunt.

◄ Named after classical composer Ludwig von **Beethoven**, the clever, if not very graceful, star proved so popular that his and his family's exploits were featured in no fewer than seven feature length sequels.

BONUS QUESTION

Name the actress who looked after a group of girls in *Girl, Interrupted* (1999), one girl in *Corrina, Corrina* (1994) and one boy in *Clara's Heart* (1988).

◄ Whoopi Goldberg

41

WHAT IS FERRIS BEULLER'S
KEY TO FAKING OUT PARENTS?

(A) A FEVER
(B) CLAMMY HANDS
(C) STOMACH CRAMPS
(D) VOMITING
(E) MOANING

► In 1986's *Ferris Bueller's Day Off*, Ferris, played by Matthew Broderick, thinks the most fool-proof way of faking sickness is **clammy hands**. "It's a good, non-specific symptom," he says, and can be achieved by simply licking your palms.

SHELLEY LONG PLAYED PHYLLIS NEFLER IN 1989'S _____, IN WHICH A PROTOTYPICAL "REAL HOUSEWIFE" BONDS WITH HER DAUGHTER AND FINDS HERSELF AMONG THE WILDERNESS GIRLS.

◄ Though unaccustomed to life in the wild, *Troop Beverly Hills* triumphs against their foes, the Culver City Red Feathers, in the ultimate cookie selling showdown.

BASED ON THE BOOK SERIES BY MICHAEL BOND, VEDDY BRITISH PADDINGTON BEAR, THE STAR OF 2014'S **PADDINGTON**, IS ORIGINALLY A NATIVE OF:

- Ⓐ PATAGONIA
- Ⓑ PORTUGAL
- Ⓒ THE PHILLIPINES
- Ⓓ PANAMA
- Ⓔ PERU

◄ Paddington hails from the deepest, darkest jungles of **Peru**, and gets his name from the famed Paddington train station in London.

Though not the only film based on a Disney theme park attraction, this film series, which began in 2003, is arguably the most popular and profitable.

BONUS QUESTION

Name the actress who was both a *Funny Girl* (1968) and a *Funny Lady* (1975).

▶ Sorry, fans of *The Haunted Mansion* (2003) and *Tomorrowland* (2015), all the **Pirates of the Caribbean** films to date, *The Curse of the Black Pearl* (2003), *Dead Man's Chest* (2006), *At World's End* (2007), and *On Stranger Tides* (2011), are so popular that animatronic versions of the films' star, Johnny Depp, have made their way into the classic theme park ride.

▶ Barbra Streisand

In the finale of 1994's

ACE VENTURA: PET DETECTIVE

the Philadelphia Eagles play the _____, whose mascot Ace was hired to find.

► Ace, played by Jim Carrey, lives and works in Miami and was hired by the Miami **Dolphins** to find its kidnapped mascot, Snowflake.

ANIMALS + FAMILY FILMS

Q True or False: *Babe: Pig in the City*, the 1998 sequel to acclaimed 1995 film *Babe*, was written and directed by *Mad Max* series creator George Miller.

Q True or False: Beloved animal adventure film *Homeward Bound: The Incredible Journey* was actually a remake of a much earlier film.

Q True or False: The soundtrack to the 1996 Muppet film *Muppet Treasure Island* was composed by famed film composer John Williams.

Q True or False: Van Pelt, the crazed hunter in *Jumanji*, is played by Jonathan Hyde, the same actor who plays Sam Parrish, the father of Alan Parrish (Robin Williams).

Q True or False: *The Parent Trap* features twin girls separated at birth, one of whom is played by Lindsay Lohan, the other played by her real-life sister Ali Lohan.

Q True or False: After playing Charlie Bucket in *Willy Wonka and the Chocolate Factory*, Peter Ostrum never acted in another film.

Q True or False: The first appearance of Danny Trejo's iconic "Machete" character took place in the family comedy *Spy Kids*.

Q True or False: Fatso, Smelly, and Stretch are the names of the "Ghostly Trio" of pranksters who haunt Whipstaff Manor in *Casper*.

A True. Miller's diverse directorial history includes a wide range of films including *Babe: Pig in the City*, *Mad Max*, *Happy Feet*, and *The Witches of Eastwick*.

A True. *Homeward Bound* was a remake of 1963's *The Incredible Journey*, which was in turn based on a novel of the same name.

A False. John Williams may not have been involved, but Hans Zimmer ensured that the music department was hardly devoid of star power.

A True. The juxtaposition of roles further underscores the disconnect between Alan and his father.

A False. In fact, both twins are played by Lindsay Lohan.

A True. Ostrum never took another film role, instead opting to become a veterinarian and eventually opening a practice in New York.

A True. Machete appears in the film as the brother of Gregorio, Antonio Banderas' character.

A False. The trio's names are Fatso, Stinkie, and Stretch.

ANIMALS + FAMILY FILMS

Q True or False: Z, the main character in *Antz*, is voiced by famously neurotic comedian Woody Allen.

Q True or False: In the movie *Hook*, Robin Williams delighted audiences with his famous portrayal of Captain Hook.

Q True or False: In 2003's *Cheaper by the Dozen*, Tom (Steve Martin) and Kate (Bonnie Hunt) move to Indiana with their 12 children so that Tom can take a job as a film producer.

Q True or False: In the 2003 remake of *Freaky Friday*, the spell that causes Anna (Lindsay Lohan) and her mother (Jamie Lee Curtis) to switch bodies is contained within a pair of fortune cookies.

Q True or False: The main character in *Holes* is named Simon, which is his last name, Nomis, spelled backwards.

Q True or False: The trick play that the team runs at the end of *Little Giants* is referred to as "The Annexation of Puerto Rico."

Q True or False: In the 1993 Disney version of *The Three Musketeers*, Tim Curry plays the devious King of Spain, who stands poised to invade France after the Musketeers are disbanded.

Q True or False: The intimidating duo of enforcers in *D2: The Mighty Ducks* are known as the "Bash Brothers."

A True. Fans of Allen's comedy will recognize many of the character's distinguishing traits.

A False. Robin Williams is indeed in the film, but he plays an older Peter Pan.

A False. Tom is a football coach and receives an offer to coach at his former college.

A True. After opening the cookies at a family dinner, Anna and her mother wake up the next day in each others' bodies.

A False. While Holes does feature a protagonist whose last name is the reverse of his first name, that character is named Stanley Yelnats.

A True. The play is a more complicated version of the famous "Fumblerooski" play.

A False. Tim Curry plays the still-devious Cardinal Richelieu, whose evil plan to undermine the throne must be thwarted by the Musketeers.

A True. Fulton Reed (Elden Henson) and Dean Portman (Aaron Lohr) quickly become inseparable.

ANIMALS + FAMILY FILMS

Q True or False: At the beginning of *Dr. Dolittle*, John's father hires a local doctor to perform a lobotomy on his son after seeing him talk to animals.

Q True or False: The movie *Beethoven* is about a giant St. Bernard dog with a miraculous talent for composing music.

Q True or False: In the superhero movie *Sky High*, sidekick training is referred to by the catchy moniker "Hero Support."

Q True or False: In the film *Air Bud*, the original owner of Buddy, the title Golden Retriever, is a clown.

Q True or False: In 2008's *Speed Racer*, Speed's iconic car is known as the Mach 10.

Q True or False: In *Cats & Dogs*, the cats' ultimate plan to defeat the dogs involves finding a way to make every human on earth allergic to dogs.

Q True or False: *Cool Runnings* centers around the unlikely success of the Mexican bobsled team at the 1988 Winter Olympics.

Q True or False: In *Lady and the Tramp*, Lady runs away from home when her family adopts a rough and tumble dog named Tramp.

Q True or False: In *The Aristocats*, Madame Bonfamille leaves her fortune to her butler, Edgar, who uses it to care for her beloved cats.

A False. Instead, his father hires a local clergyman to perform an exorcism.

A False. Beethoven is about a St. Bernard, but sadly not one capable of musical expression.

A True. Students without useful superpowers are relegated to "Hero Support" to aid more capable heroes.

A True. Norm Snively, known by his clown name "Happy Slappy," attempts to regain custody of Buddy after learning about his unique skill set.

A False. Speed (Emile Hirsch) drives the Mach 5, and, later on, the Mach 6.

A True. The cats plan to use research conducted by Professor Brody (Jeff Goldblum) on curing dog allergies.

A False. The bobsled team in *Cool Runnings* hails from the equally-warm country of Jamaica.

A False. Lady does flee home, but she does so after being mistreated by her temporary caretaker when the family leaves for a vacation.

A False. Madame Bonfamille plans to leave her entire fortune to her cats, which enrages Edgar and spurs him to kidnap the cats.

FANTASY and SCIENCE FICTION

A long time ago, these films boldly went to places and spaces never imagined—but hopefully remembered!

IN 1980'S

STAR WARS EPISODE V: THE EMPIRE STRIKES BACK

LUKE SKYWALKER LOSES HIS _____ IN A FIGHT WITH DARTH VADER.

▶ Vader and Luke's father/son relationship got off to a rocky start in Cloud City when, during their lightsaber duel, Vader removes his son's **right hand.**

Name all of the Harry Potter films in their chronological order.

Harry Potter and the Deathly Hallows: Part 2 (2011)
Harry Potter and the Deathly Hallows: Part 1 (2010)
Harry Potter and the Half-Blood Prince (2009)
Harry Potter and the Order of the Phoenix (2007)
Harry Potter and the Goblet of Fire (2005)
Harry Potter and the Prisoner of Azkaban (2004)
Harry Potter and the Chamber of Secrets (2002)
▶ Harry Potter and the Sorcerer's Stone (2001)

BONUS QUESTION

Name the director of such testosterone-filled films as *The Hurt Locker* (2008) and *Zero Dark Thirty* (2012).

▶ Kathryn Bigelow

WHEN DAVID LYNCH ADAPTED _____,
HE CAST A POPULAR AND AWARD-WINNING
MUSICIAN IN A ROLE THAT WAS, IN THE BOOK,
DESCRIBED AS BEING JUST 16 YEARS OLD.

- Ⓐ **THE JAZZ SINGER**
- Ⓑ **DUNE**
- Ⓒ **LABYRINTH**
- Ⓓ **MASK**
- Ⓔ **PURPLE RAIN**

▶ Sting was in his early 30s when he starred as Feyd-Rautha Harkonnen in the film adaptation of Frank Herbert's *Dune*.

FALKOR THE LUCKDRAGON
IS NOT ONLY A TRUSTY FRIEND,
BUT A RELIABLE MEANS OF
TRANSPORTATION AROUND
FANTASIA IN _____.

▶ 1984's *The Neverending Story* introduced audiences to a world created by author Michael Ende. Ironically, the film series ended after 1990's *The Neverending Story II: The Next Chapter* and 1994's *The Neverending Story III: Escape from Fantasia*.

MORPHEUS OFFERS THOMAS ANDERSON TWO PILLS. ONE WILL SHOW HIM THE TRUTH, THE OTHER WILL LET HIM CONTINUE LIVING AS HE HAD BEEN. HE CHOOSES THE _____ ONE.

▶ In the Wachowski's 1999 film, Anderson, also known as "Neo," played by Keanu Reeves, pops the **red** pill into his mouth and becomes aware of the truth surrounding *The Matrix*.

NAME THE TWO RACES THAT JOIN TOGETHER WHEN **THE DARK CRYSTAL** IS RESTORED.

▶ **The Mystics and the Skeksis**, two halves of a whole, are brought back together when the three suns align in Jim Henson and Frank Oz's 1982 non-Muppety but puppety live action film.

BEFORE THEY'RE RALLIED TO STORM THE LONELY MOUNTAIN, ORCS CALLED THESE TWO PLACES HOME IN 2014'S

THE HOBBIT: THE BATTLE OF THE FIVE ARMIES:

A GUNDABAD

B RIVENDELL

C DOL GULDUR

D EREBOR

E PARAMUS

▶ Azog led the orcs from **Dol Guldur**, while Bolg led those from **Gundabad** against the elves, dwarves, and men in the final installment of director Peter Jackson's prequel trilogy.

UNLIKE HIS ROLES IN SUCH
FILMS AND TELEVISION SHOWS AS
GOLDENEYE,
THE LORD OF THE RINGS,
AND "GAME OF THRONES," SEAN BEAN'S
CHARACTER DOES NOT DIE IN _____,
THE WACHOWSKI'S 2014 SPACE OPERA.

► Unlike many critics and fans, Sean Bean's Stinger Apini, a half-human/half-honeybee makes it to the end of *Jupiter Ascending*.

JOHN CARTER
TAKES PLACE ON EARTH
AND BARSOOM OR,
AS WE LIKE TO CALL IT,

_____.

► Based on the "Barsoom" series of books by Edgar Rice Burrows, who was also the creator of jungle-dwelling Tarzan, the 2012 film starring Taylor Kitsch takes place mostly on **Mars**.

IN 1981'S
CLASH OF THE TITANS,

PERSEUS USES _____'S HEAD TO TURN THE CRACKEN TO STONE.

CALIBOS

MEDUSA

CASSIOPEIA

AMMON

or ATHENA

▶ According to myth, Athena turned **Medusa** into a hideous creature with snakes for hair whose very look would turn people to stone. Clever Perseus, played by Harry Hamlin in 1981 and Sam Worthington in 2010, uses reflective surfaces to find, and slay, the gorgon.

YOU MIGHT RECALL THAT THOUGH KUATO HAS A LOT OF HEART AND BRAINS, HE CAN BE FOUND

▶ Arnold Schwarzenegger's Quaid, along with audiences everywhere, searched for the leader of the resistance in 1990's *Total Recall*, only to find him **attached to his brother's stomach.**

JOSH BROLIN, WHO PLAYS PURPLE-SKINNED BADDIE THANOS IN MANY MARVEL CINEMATIC UNIVERSE MOVIES, PLAYS SHARPLY DRESSED GOODIE _____, IN THE THIRD INSTALLMENT OF A FILM FRANCHISE.

▶ Brolin plays a younger version of Agent K in *Men in Black 3* (2012), played by Tommy Lee Jones in *Men in Black* (1997), and *Men in Black 2* (2002).

THOUGH SIMILAR-SOUNDING TO A ROCK-AND-ROLLER'S, THESE GIANT, ROBOT-LIKE SUITS WERE CONTROLLED BY TWO PEOPLE, NOT A BACK-UP BAND, IN 2013'S **PACIFIC RIM**:

A RICKARDS
B JAEGERS
C MCPARTNEYS
D LEMMONS
E BIEBERS

▶ The **Jaegers** didn't have "Sticky Fingers" when they hit a kaiju "Between the Buttons," and other weak spots, leaving it to "Let it Bleed" in the "Aftermath," and they certainly got a lot of "Satisfaction" when the monsters kaiju were "Exile[d] on Main St." and elsewhere.

PERHAPS INSPIRED BY A MYTHOLOGICAL PRINCESS, ELLEN PAGE'S CHARACTER IN CHRISTOPHER NOLAN'S 2010 **INCEPTION**, IS NAMED

_____.

▶ **Ariadne**, who is charged by her father to oversee the labyrinth containing the Minotaur, may have inspired Nolan to create Page's character, an architecture student hired by Leonardo DiCaprio's Cobb to create dreamscapes.

NAME THE CORRECT PHRASE FROM 2009'S **AVATAR**:

- **A** I HEAR YOU
- **B** I FEEL YOU
- **C** I TASTE YOU
- **D** I SEE YOU
- **E** I SMELL YOU

▶ **Na'vi, humans, and audiences alike were moved by the sentiment behind "I see you," which can be a greeting, but also a declaration that one being truly understands and embraces what is before them.**

In 1973's
SOYLENT GREEN,
"Soylent Green" is green.
It is also _____.

▶ **The story of an** overpopulated world in which people fight for survival, the Soylent Corporation tells everyone that their new superfood is derived from plankton when it is, in fact, **people!**

AUDIENCES COULD WATCH, AND REWATCH, TOM CRUISE RELIVE THE SAME DAY OVER AND OVER AGAIN, BUT WERE CONFUSED BY THE TITLE OF 2014'S **EDGE OF TOMORROW**. TO CLARIFY THINGS, SUBSEQUENT VIDEO AND ON DEMAND RELEASES TOUTED IT WITH ITS UNOFFICIAL SUBTITLE, _____.

► The film, in which Tom Cruise *Groundhog Day*'s his way through a war with Emily Blunt, was rebranded as "Live. Die. Repeat."

PICK THE CORRECT BILL/QUAID PAIR WHO STARRED IN **INDEPENDENCE DAY**:

- **A** BILL PULLMAN AND RANDY QUAID
- **B** BILL PAXTON AND RANDY QUAID
- **C** BILL PULLMAN AND DENNIS QUAID
- **D** BILL PAXTON AND DENNIS QUAID
- **E** BILL PULLMAN AND JACK QUAID

► The 1996 film starred **Bill Pullman and Randy Quaid**, along with Will Smith, Jeff Goldblum, and Margaret Colin.

IN PETER JACKSON'S

KING KONG,

THIS ACTOR DOES DOUBLE DUTY AS BOTH THE TITLE CHARACTER AND THE SHIP'S CHEF, LUMPY.

► **Andy Serkis,** whose performance capture work as Gollum in the *Lord of the Rings* and *Hobbit* movies solidified his and Jackson's working relationship, played both the CGI giant gorilla and the ill-fated seaman in the 2005 remake of the 1933 classic.

BONUS QUESTION

Show your "jazz hands" and name the director of *Cabaret* (1972) and *All That Jazz* (1979).

► Bob Fosse

63

IN 1977'S

CLOSE ENCOUNTERS OF THE THIRD KIND,

ROY NEARY BUILDS A MODEL OF DEVILS TOWER OUT OF _____.

▶ The character, played by Richard Dreyfuss, who came sunburned, face-to-face with UFOs, finds inspiration to visit the natural landmark in his mashed potatoes.

THE EGYPTIAN GOD _____ ISN'T A GOD, BUT AN ALIEN IN 1994'S **STARGATE**.

► Played by Jaye Davidson, Ra, once worshiped as the Sun God, turns out to be a megalomaniacal alien bent on the destruction of humankind.

ALLUSIONS TO **PINOCCHIO** MAKE THEIR WAY THROUGHOUT _____, ESPECIALLY WHEN DAVID ENCOUNTERS HIS VERY OWN BLUE ANGEL.

► Steven Spielberg took the directing reins from Stanley Kubrik on 2001's **A.I. Artificial Intelligence**, in which Haley Joel Osment portrays David, a robot boy programmed to love.

IN 2005'S
WAR OF THE WORLDS,
TOM CRUISE'S
RAY FERRIER TRIES
TO GET HIS FAMILY TO:

A NEW YORK CITY

B BOSTON

C PROVIDENCE

D BUFFALO

E PORTLAND

▶ Ray tries to deliver his children, Rachel and Robbie (played by Dakota Fanning and Justin Chatwin), through alien forces and to their mother, played by Miranda Otto, in **Boston.**

2012, A FILM DIRECTED BY ROLAND EMMERICH IN WHICH NATURAL DISASTERS THREATEN ALL OF HUMAN EXISTENCE, PREMIERED A MERE EIGHT YEARS AFTER _____ HIT THEATERS, ANOTHER FILM DIRECTED BY ROLAND EMMERICH IN WHICH A NEW ICE AGE THREATENS ALL OF HUMAN EXISTENCE.

◄ *2012*, starring John Cusack and Chiwetel Ejiofor, came out in 2009, many days after 2004's *The Day After Tomorrow*, starring Dennis Quaid and Jake Gyllenhaal.

ARMAGEDDON CAME OUT THE SAME YEAR AS THIS SIMILARLY THEMED DISASTER FILM:

- **A** **DEEP IMPACT**
- **B** **THE CORE**
- **C** **METEOR**
- **D** **VOLCANO**
- **E** **DANTE'S PEAK**

◄ Almost 20 years after *Meteor* hit theatres in 1979, both *Armageddon* and *Deep Impact* made, well, an impact with audiences in 1998. Lava flowed a lot in 1997's *Dante's Peak* and *Volcano*, while Hilary Swank lead an expedition into *The Core of the Earth* in 2003.

FANTASY + SCIENCE FICTION

Q True or False: Fans of the comics on which it was based were unhappy with Sylvester Stallone's refusal to remove his helmet in the movie *Judge Dredd*.

Q True or False: In post-apocalyptic classic *Mad Max 2: The Road Warrior*, a band of marauders is attempting to overrun a water treatment plant in the middle of the wasteland.

Q True or False: Bruce Willis' character in science fiction epic *The Fifth Element* works as a taxi driver.

Q True or False: In 2003, *The Return of the King*, the final installment in Peter Jackson's *Lord of the Rings* trilogy, won all 11 Academy Awards for which it was nominated.

Q True or False: In *Escape from New York*, the entirety of Manhattan Island has been converted into one gigantic prison.

Q True or False: The androids who serve as the antagonists in *Blade Runner* are robotic creations known as "replicants."

Q True or False: In *Contact*, the alien message detected by Ellie Arroway (Jodie Foster) is broadcast in 10 of the most widely spoken Earth languages.

Q True or False: *District 9* was the directorial debut of Neill Blomkamp.

Q True or False: In *Children of Men*, all of humanity has become sterile following a terrible nuclear war.

A False. In fact, it was just the opposite: despite a character who famously never removes his helmet, Stallone spent the majority of the film with his head uncovered.

A False. While water is an important resource in Max's world, it is an oil refinery at the heart of automotively inclined *The Road Warrior*.

A True. Korben Dallas, played by Bruce Willis, is a disgruntled taxi driver at the end of his rope.

A True. The film is tied with *Ben-Hur* and *Titanic* for the largest number of Academy Awards won.

A True. The entire island is surrounded by a 50-foot wall to prevent escape.

A True. Manufactured by the Tyrell Corporation, replicants are designed to be visually identical to humans.

A False. The message is devoid of words of any kind, instead coming in the form of mathematics.

A True. Although Blomkamp had directed some short films, *District 9* was the first time he helmed a feature film.

A False. In the film, nobody knows why the human race suddenly lost the ability to produce children.

FANTASY + SCIENCE FICTION

Q True or False: In *Highlander*, the only way to kill an immortal like Connor MacLeod (Christopher Lambert) is to stab him or her in the heart.

Q True or False: Clint Eastwood was originally offered the role of Agent K of the *Men in Black* franchise.

Q True or False: In *Back to the Future Part II*, Michael J. Fox plays his character's future self, as well as both of his future children.

Q True or False: Ridley Scott, James Cameron, and David Fincher have all directed films in the *Alien* franchise.

Q True or False: In 2009's *Moon*, GERTY, the robot companion who assists Sam Bell (Sam Rockwell), is voiced by the famously monotonous Ben Stein.

Q True or False: In *A Clockwork Orange*, Alex DeLarge refers to his band of followers as "droogs."

Q True or False: The fairy tale at the heart of *Pan's Labyrinth* is centered around the daughter of the Lord of the Underworld.

Q True or False: Although *The Lion, the Witch, and the Wardrobe* was the first film in the series, it is based on the second book in C.S. Lewis' famous *Chronicles of Narnia*.

A False. Nothing short of complete decapitation can kill an immortal.

A True. Tommy Lee Jones would play the role in the movies.

A True. Fox plays Marty McFly in two different time periods, as well as his twin son and daughter.

A True. Scott directed *Alien*, Cameron directed *Aliens*, and Fincher directed *Alien 3*.

A False. GERTY is voiced by Kevin Spacey.

A True. The movie is filled with made-up words and creative language.

A True. Princess Moanna, the daughter of the Lord of the Underworld, loses her memories when she visits the human realm.

A True. Although *The Lion, the Witch, and the Wardrobe* was the first book to be published, it was actually the second book chronologically.

FANTASY + SCIENCE FICTION

Q True or False: The plot of *Stardust* revolves around a magical region known as the Starlands.

Q True or False: In *Her*, Theodore Twombly (Joaquin Phoenix) purchases and befriends an intelligent operating system voiced by Emma Stone.

Q True or False: To prevent them from breeding out of control, every dinosaur in *Jurassic Park* is genetically engineered to be male.

Q True or False: In *Army of Darkness*, the book that Ash needs to find in order to return to his own time is the legendary Necronomicon.

Q True or False: The title of the film *Serenity* refers to the home planet of protagonist Malcolm Reynolds (Nathan Fillion).

Q True or False: In *Star Trek IV: The Voyage Home*, Captain Kirk (William Shatner) and his crew must stop an attack on earth by going back in time to retrieve a pair of humpback whales.

Q True or False: Arnold Schwarzenegger's famous "Get to the chopper!" line is spoken during the movie *Predator*.

Q True or False: The war with the Arachnids in *Starship Troopers* begins when the Arachnids attack earth with a new, shockingly advanced spaceship.

A False. The magical kingdom is known as Stormhold.

A False. The operating system is voiced by Scarlett Johansson.

A False. The dinosaurs are all female, hence the famous "clever girl" line, spoken by Robert Muldoon in reference to one of the park's velociraptors.

A True. The book that caused so much trouble in the first two installments of the *Evil Dead* series again surfaces in *Army of Darkness*.

A False. Serenity is the name of the ship owned by the movie's protagonists.

A True. Although it sounds like an odd plot device for a science fiction movie, the crew returns to 1986 San Francisco in search of whales.

A True. Ironically, the actor who played the helicopter pilot also had another role in the film: the titular Predator himself.

A False. The war begins when the Arachnids launch an asteroid at the earth, which collides with Buenos Aires.

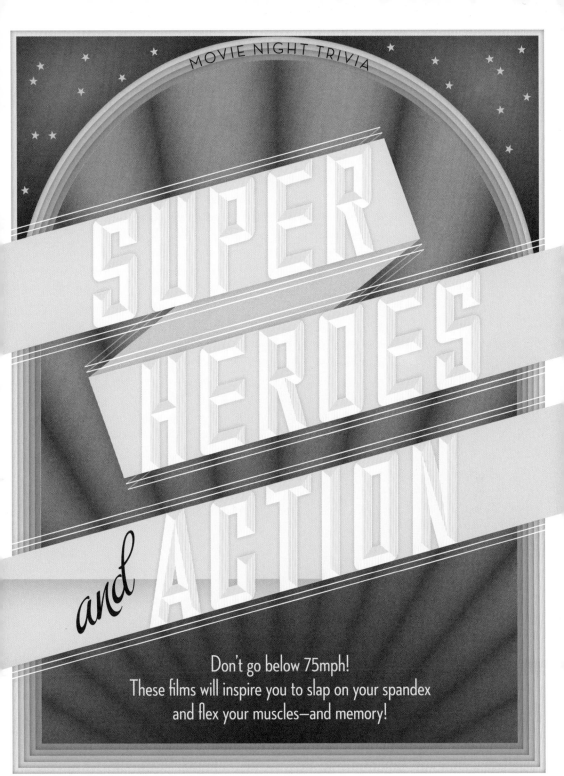

IN 2013'S **MAN OF STEEL**, GENERAL ZOD ATTEMPTS TO TERRAFORM EARTH INTO A NEW KRYPTON BY DEPLOYING WORLD ENGINES TO METROPOLIS AND _____.

▶ While Lois Lane, Colonel Hardy, and Dr. Hamilton (played by Amy Adams, Christopher Meloni, and Richard Schiff) deal with the machine hanging over Metropolis, Superman (played by Henry Cavill) rushes to destroy the one causing havoc in the **Indian Ocean**.

WHICH OF THESE IS NOT A MEMBER OF THE **WATCHMEN**:

- **A** DR. MANHATTAN
- **B** OZYMANDIAS
- **C** SILK SPECTRE
- **D** THE COMEDIAN
- **E** MOLOCH

▶ **Moloch**, played by Matt Frewer, is a nemesis of Nite Owl, played by Patrick Wilson. Though retired from villainy, he was never on the side of good (or good-ish) with the Watchmen, played in the 2009 film by Billy Crudup, Matthew Goode, Malin Ackerman, and Jeffrey Dean Morgan.

THE NAME OF THIS CLASSIC CHARACTER IS NEVER MENTIONED IN 2012'S

THE DARK KNIGHT RISES:

- **A** BATMAN
- **B** BANE
- **C** ROBIN
- **D** ALFRED
- **E** CATWOMAN

► Though a cat burglar, Anne Hathaway's Selina Kyle is never formally identified as **Catwoman**, who first made her debut in 1940's Batman #1 comic book.

THOUGH NONE WOULD REPRISE THEIR ROLES IN THE SIMILARLY THEMED JULIE TAYMOR-DIRECTED BROADWAY MUSICAL, DIRECTOR SAM RAIMI'S 2004 _____ FEATURED NO FEWER THAN FOUR WELL-KNOWN BROADWAY STARS.

▶ *Spider-Man 2* starred Tony Award nominees and winners Alfred Molina as Doctor Otto Octavius/Doctor Octopus, Rosemary Harris as Aunt May Parker, J.K. Simmons as J. Jonah Jameson, and Donna Murphy as Rosalie Octavius.

NAME THE ONLY CHARACTER FROM THE 1978-1987 **SUPERMAN** MOVIES TO MAKE AN APPEARANCE IN 1984'S **SUPERGIRL**.

▶ Superman's pal, **Jimmy Olsen**, played by Marc McClure in *Superman* (1978), *Superman II* (1980), *Superman III* (1983), and *Superman IV: The Quest for Peace* (1987), was the only character and actor to make an appearance in the spin-off film starring Helen Slater and Faye Dunaway.

THOUGH AS PATRIOTIC AS APPLE PIE, IN **CAPTAIN AMERICA: THE FIRST AVENGER**, STEVE ROGERS (CHRIS EVANS) FALLS FOR A WOMAN FROM _____.

▶ Proving that love knows no borders, Steve falls for an agent from **The United Kingdom** named **Peggy** Carter in the 2011 film. The character, played by Hayley Atwell, proved so popular with fans (and not just superheroes) that she is now the star of her own titular television series premiering in 2015.

NAME THE TELEVISION STAR FEATURED ON HARLEY'S SISTER'S WATCH IN 2013'S **IRON MAN 3**:

A DOC MCSTUFFINS

B RAINBOW BRITE

C DORA THE EXPLORER

D SOFIA THE FIRST

E SMURFETTE

▶ Though he tries to dissuade them, Tony Stark's captors destroy the prized **Dora the Explorer** timepiece. But because he is a super-rich superhero, he manages to find a replacement by the end of the movie.

MATCH THE ACTOR
TO THE CHARACTER FROM 2014'S
GUARDIANS OF THE GALAXY

BENICIO DEL TORO	RHOMANN DEY
MICHAEL ROOKER	THE COLLECTOR
PETER SERAFINOWICZ	THE BROKER
JOHN C. REILLY	YONDU UDONTA
CHRISTOPHER FAIRBANK	DENARIAN SAAL

Michael Rooker: Yondu Udonta

Benicio del Toro: The Collector

Christopher Fairbank: The Broker

John C. Reilly: Rhomann Dey

confusing names:

Peter Serafinowicz: Denarian Saal

Universe, is filled with lots of stars and lots of

► Outer space, and the Marvel Cinematic

WHAT SOUTH AMERICAN COUNTRY DOES ERIK LEHNSHERR TRAVEL TO IN ORDER TO EXACT REVENGE ON NAZIS WHO ESCAPED PROSECUTION IN 2011'S **X-MEN: FIRST CLASS**?

► Erik, later known as Magneto and played by Michael Fassbender, finds the outlaws in **Argentina**, where he gets his revenge before seeking out Kevin Bacon's Klaus Schmidt.

NAME THE AUSTRALIAN ACTOR WHO PORTRAYED A DOCTOR WITH RAGE ISSUES IN A 2003 FILM DIRECTED BY ANG LEE BEFORE HANDING OVER THE PURPLE PANTS TO TWO OTHER ACTORS IN THREE SUBSEQUENT MOVIES.

► **Eric Bana** was the first actor to play Bruce Banner in *Hulk*. Edward Norton followed in his rampaging footsteps in 2008's *The Incredible Hulk*, followed by Mark Ruffalo in 2012's *The Avengers* and 2015's *Avengers: Age of Ultron*.

IN 2007'S **FANTASTIC 4:
RISE OF THE SILVER SURFER**,
THE SILVER SURFER IS A HARBINGER
OF WHAT EVIL ENTITY:

A THANOS

B DARKSEID

C GALACTUS

D PARALLAX

E ANNIHILUS

◄ Norrin Radd, also known as The Silver Surfer, embodied by Doug Jones and voiced by Laurence Fishburn, heralds the coming of **Galactus**, who is determined to destroy the Earth.

BEFORE STARRING AS
THE TITULAR HERO IN DIRECTOR
MARTIN CAMPBELL'S 2011 FILM
GREEN LANTERN,
RYAN REYNOLDS PORTRAYED
_____ IN 2009'S **X-MEN
ORIGINS: WOLVERINE**.

◄ Before making the move to comic book rival DC Entertainment, Reynolds starred as Marvel Comics' **Deadpool**.

IN 2011'S THOR, HEIMDALL CAN SEE ALL OF THE NINE REALMS, INCLUDING HEL, JOTUNHEIM, SVARTALFHEIM, AND ____, WHAT WE CALL EARTH.

▶ Though Loki may escape the watchful gaze of the sentry of the Bifrost, played by Idris Elba, Heimdall can see all the way to **Midgard**, where Thor (Chris Hemsworth) meets and falls in love with Jane Foster (Natalie Portman).

ARMIE HAMMER PLAYS A NEWLY-DEPUTIZED, ONLY SURVIVOR OF A RAID ON LAWMEN IN WHAT 2013 WESTERN?

▶ Encouraged by Johnny Depp's Tonto and driven to seek justice, Hammer's John Reid straps on a mask and becomes **The Lone Ranger.**

WHICH FAMOUS LITERARY CHARACTER DOES NOT APPEAR IN 2003'S THE LEAGUE OF EXTRAORDINARY GENTLEMEN:

A MINA HARKER

B DORIAN GRAY

C DR. JEKYLL

D CAPTAIN NEMO

E HUCKLEBERRY FINN

▶ Based on Alan Moore and Kevin O'Neil's comic book series, the film starred Peta Wilson as Mina, Stuart Townsend as Dorian, Jason Flemyng as Jekyll, and Naseeruddin Shah as Captain Nemo. It added Shane West as Tom Sawyer, not **Huckleberry Finn**, as the only American to its roster of classic heroes.

MARKETED WITH THE TAGLINE "THE BAT. THE CAT. THE PENGUIN."

THIS 1992 FILM IS CONSIDERED BY SOME TO BE THE FIRST SUPERHERO CHRISTMAS MOVIE.

► Tim Burton's sequel to 1989's *Batman*, *Batman Returns* starred Michelle Pfeiffer as Catwoman and Danny DeVito as The Penguin, both of whom tried to make the holidays difficult for Batman, played again by Michael Keaton, and Max Schreck, whose lighting of the Gotham Christmas Tree is interrupted by a plummeting Ice Princess and rampaging circus performers.

BONUS QUESTION

Name the actor/director who sang in *High Anxiety* (1977) but didn't say a word in *Silent Movie* (1976).

► Mel Brooks

83

PUT THE SEVEN
FAST & FURIOUS
MOVIES IN THEIR IN-WORLD ORDER:

THE FAST AND THE FURIOUS
2 FAST 2 FURIOUS
THE FAST AND THE FURIOUS: TOKYO DRIFT
FAST & FURIOUS
FAST FIVE
FAST AND FURIOUS 6
FURIOUS 7

► *The Fast and the Furious: Tokyo Drift*, the third film in the series (and first directed by Justin Lin), actually takes place after *Fast & Furious 6*, the last film he directed. Lin also directed *Fast and Furious*, the fourth film in the series, and *Fast Five*, while the others were helmed by directors Rob Cohen (*The Fast and Furious*), John Singleton (*2 Fast 2 Furious*), and James Wan (*Furious 7*).

BONUS QUESTION

Name the director who directed his actor father, Walter, to an Oscar for 1948's *The Treasure of the Sierra Madre* and his actress daughter, Angelica, to an Oscar for 1985's *Prizzi's Honor*.

► John Huston

84

Name the 2004 film, written and directed by Guillermo del Toro, in which an infant demon grows up to join the BPRD.

▶ Ron Perlman plays the adult *Hellboy*, who works for the Bureau of Paranormal Research and Defense, along with Abe Sapien and Liz Sherman, played by Doug Jones and Selma Blair.

BONUS QUESTION

Name the actress who lived on a mountain as *Heidi* (1937) and on a farm as *Rebecca of Sunnybrook Farm* (1938).

▶ Shirley Temple

WHICH ACTOR DID NOT APPEAR IN 2012'S **THE EXPENDABLES 2**?

A JEAN-CLAUDE VAN DAMME

B BRUCE WILLIS

C CHUCK NORRIS

D HARRISON FORD

E WESLEY SNIPES

► Though he appeared in all three Blade films, Blade (1998), Blade II (2002), and Blade: Trinity (2004), **Wesley Snipes** has only appeared in one Expendables movie to date, 2014's The Expendables 3.

IN 2006'S **300**, GERARD BUTLER'S KING LEONIDAS LEADS WHICH ARMY INTO BATTLE AGAINST THE PERSIAN GOD KING?

► Based on the comic book series by Frank Miller and Lynn Varley, the movie is a fictionalized tale of the Battle of Thermopylae, in which 300 **Spartan** soldiers fought a losing battle against the larger Persian army.

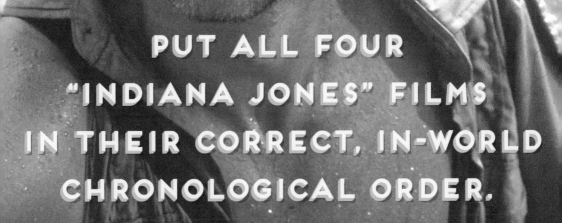

PUT ALL FOUR
"INDIANA JONES" FILMS
IN THEIR CORRECT, IN-WORLD
CHRONOLOGICAL ORDER.

► Taking place in 1935, *Indiana Jones and the Temple of Doom*, released in 1984, the second film in the franchise, is a prequel to *Raiders of the Lost Ark*, the series' first film, which was released in 1981 and takes place in 1936. The series continues with 1989's *Indiana Jones and the Last Crusade* and 2008's *Indiana Jones and the Kingdom of the Crystal Skull*.

Based on a series of books by Robert Ludlum, this 2002 film started a movie franchise that switched main characters in the fourth film.

BONUS QUESTION

Name the actress who starred as Effie alongside Rosalind Russell in 1942's *My Sister Eileen* and was the inspiration for the character Baby June in 1962's *Gypsy*, starring Rosalind Russell.

◄ June Havoc

◄ Matt Damon starred in *The Bourne Identity*, 2004's *The Bourne Supremacy*, and 2007's *The Bourne Ultimatum* before handing over the reins to Jeremy Renner in 2012's *The Bourne Legacy*.

2003'S **THE ITALIAN JOB**

STARRED MARK WAHLBERG, CHARLIZE THERON, DONALD SUTHERLAND, JASON STATHAM, AND WHICH POPULAR BRAND OF CARS?

A **FIATS**

B **MINI COOPERS**

C **ASTON MARTINS**

D **BMWS**

E **VW BEETLES**

► As in the original 1969 film, which starred Michael Caine, Benny Hill, and Noel Coward, Mini Coopers play a prominent role in the films' main heist scenes.

BONUS QUESTION

Name the actor who engaged in *Pillow Talk* with Doris Day (1959) and a *Showdown* with Dean Martin (1973).

► Rock Hudson

NAME BRUCE LEE'S LAST FILM.

▶ 1973's *Enter the Dragon* was released just after Lee died.

Add the following:
The number of men to have played James Bond in official feature films to date, plus the number of films called

CASINO ROYALE, plus 007.

◄ 6: (Sean Connery in Dr. No, From Russia with Love, Goldfinger, Thunderball, You Only Live Twice, Diamonds Are Forever, and Never Say Never Again) George Lazenby in On Her Majesty's Secret Service Roger Moore in Live and Let Die, The Man with the Golden Gun, The Spy Who Loved Me, Moonraker, For Your Eyes Only, Octopussy, and A View to a Kill) Timothy Dalton in The Living Daylights and License to Kill) Pierce Brosnan in Golden Eye, Tomorrow Never Dies, The World is Not Enough, and Die Another Day Daniel Craig in Casino Royale, Quantum of Solace, and Skyfall) Plus 2: (David Niven's Casino Royale in 1967 and Daniel Craig's in 2006) Plus 007 Equals 15.

SUPERHEROES + ACTION

Q True or False: *Die Hard* is regarded as one of the most patriotic films of all time, with its action taking place on the 4th of July.

Q True or False: Guy Ritchie's *Snatch* features characters with strange nicknames, including "Brick Top," "Bullet-Tooth," and "The Bullet Dodger."

Q True or False: The classic 1987 buddy cop film *Lethal Weapon* features an unusual pair of police detectives played by Bruce Willis and Samuel L. Jackson.

Q True or False: Chris O'Donnell, who played the role of Batman's sidekick Robin in *Batman Forever*, was the first actor to play Robin on the big screen.

Q True or False: In 2002's *Spider-Man*, Spider-Man's webs are organic, while in 2012's *The Amazing Spider-Man*, he uses mechanical web shooters.

Q True or False: In the film reboot of *The A-Team*, the team is put at odds with an unscrupulous CIA agent who goes by the codename "Lynch."

Q True or False: In a last-ditch attempt to put an end to the alien invasion in *The Avengers*, a nuclear missile is launched at New York City.

Q True or False: In *The Dark Knight*, Harvey Dent (Aaron Eckhart) survives the Joker's assassination attempt after Batman chooses to save him over his friend Rachel Dawes (Maggie Gyllenhaal).

A False. *Die Hard* actually takes place around Christmas, and is considered by some to be a sort of Christmas movie.

A True. Brick Top, Bullet-Tooth Tony, and Boris the Bullet Dodger are all characters in the 2000 gangster comedy.

A False. Detectives Riggs and Murtaugh are played by Mel Gibson and Danny Glover, respectively; however, Willis and Jackson would later team up in the third *Die Hard* installment, *Die Hard with a Vengeance*.

A False. Actor Douglas Croft was the first to play Robin all the way back in 1943's *Batman*.

A True. Although most iterations of Spider-Man involve mechanical web shooters, *Spider-Man* director Sam Raimi felt that it would be difficult for audiences to take seriously.

A True. It is heavily implied that "Lynch" is the default codename used by CIA agents.

A True. Thankfully, the heroes are able to redirect the missile for their own purposes.

A False. Batman does save Dent's life, but only after the Joker tricks him into believing that Rachel would be at Dent's location.

SUPERHEROES + ACTION

Q True or False: The 2014 superhero romp *Guardians of the Galaxy* features a talking dog named Rocket.

Q True or False: Nicolas Cage's character in 2010's *Kick-Ass* goes by the name "Big Daddy."

Q True or False: *Never Say Never Again*, Sean Connery's return to the role of James Bond, was a reboot of earlier Bond film *Thunderball*.

Q True or False: *The Crow* was the final movie of lead actor Brandon Lee.

Q True or False: In *Unbreakable*, David Dunn (Bruce Willis) first begins to suspect that he has unique powers when he is the sole survivor of a plane crash.

Q True or False: At the beginning of *X2: X-Men United*, the prison cell in which Magneto (Ian McKellan) is imprisoned is made entirely of plastic.

Q True or False: In 2005's *Sin City*, the character of Dwight McCarthy is played by Clive Owen, while in the 2014 follow-up film *Sin City: A Dame to Kill For*, the character is played by Josh Brolin.

Q True or False: *Gladiator* features Russell Crowe as the legendary Roman general Gladius, who is betrayed and forced to fight as a Gladiator.

Q True or False: In the movie *Speed*, a terrorist rigs a bus to explode if its speed drops below 88 miles per hour.

A False. Rocket is not a dog, but a precocious raccoon.

A True. Big Daddy is the father of Hit-Girl (Chloë Grace Moretz), the sometimes-ally of Kick-Ass (Aaron Taylor-Johnson).

A True. Connery stepped away from the role for 12 years, famously declaring that he would "never" play the part again.

A True. Lee was tragically killed in an accident during filming. The finished film is dedicated to him and his fiancée.

A False. Dunn survives a major train crash, not a plane crash.

A True. To prevent Magneto from using his power over metal to escape, the cell is specially constructed using only plastics.

A True. In *Sin City*, McCarthy references his "new face," making the substitution an easy one to swallow.

A False. Crowe's character is General Maximus, a role for which he won the Academy Award for Best Actor.

A False. The bus only has to stay above 50 MPH. 88 MPH is, of course, the speed necessary for time travel in *Back to the Future*.

SUPERHEROES + ACTION

Q True or False: Frank Costello (Jack Nicholson), the villainous crime boss in *The Departed*, is loosely based on famous Boston mobster Whitey Bulger.

Q True or False: The protagonist in *V for Vendetta* is a vigilante who hides his identity behind a Richard Nixon mask.

Q True or False: The MacManus Brothers, the protagonists of *The Boondock Saints*, each have one of the Latin words for "truth" and "justice" tattooed on their hands.

Q True or False: In the film *John Wick*, Keanu Reeves' titular character goes on a rampage when his former employer's son unknowingly kills his wife.

Q True or False: The Clint Eastwood catchphrase "go ahead, make my day" originated in 1971's *Dirty Harry*.

Q True or False: Antonio Banderas, who played El Mariachi in the films *Desperado* and *Once Upon a Time in Mexico*, was not the first actor to play the role.

Q True or False: In *The Rock*, John Mason (Sean Connery) and Stanley Goodspeed (Nicolas Cage) are enlisted to help defeat a former general who has taken over the famous Riker's Island Prison in New York.

Q True or False: In *Django Unchained*, Django (Jamie Foxx) is searching for his long-lost wife, named Broomhilda.

A True. In 2011, just five years after the film's 2006 release, Bulger was finally arrested after 16 years on the run.

A False. V hides his face behind a Guy Fawkes mask, a symbol that gained considerable popularity in the wake of the film.

A True. Connor MacManus (Sean Patrick Flannery) has "veritas" (truth) tattooed on his left hand, while Murphy MacManus (Norman Reedus) has "aequitas" (justice) tattooed on his right hand.

A False. Although Wick's wife is dead in the film, the action kicks off when the gangster's son kills his dog.

A False. Although it was indeed Harry Callahan who spoke the line, it wasn't spoken until 1983's *Sudden Impact*, the fourth film in the *Dirty Harry* series.

A True. Banderas took over for Carlos Gallardo, the actor who played the role in the first film in Robert Rodriguez's *Mexico Trilogy, El Mariachi*.

A False. *The Rock* does take place in an island prison, but that prison is Alcatraz.

A True. Dr. King Schultz (Christoph Waltz) helps Django in exchange for his help collecting a bounty.

DRAMA

and CLASSICS

Hope your tissue box is filled! These films will get
your tear ducts, and brains, working overdrive!

IN 1997'S

TITANIC,

KATHY BATES PORTRAYED

—————————————————,

A PASSENGER WHO
WAS THE SUBJECT OF
HER OWN 1964 FILM.

◄ Debbie Reynolds played the title character in *The Unsinkable Molly Brown*, a musical retelling
of the life and times of one of the few survivors of the 1912 disaster.

What do the main characters in 1969's

EASY RIDER

ride?

Bicycles
Unicycles
Motorcycles
Mopeds
Segways

BONUS QUESTION

Name the actor who played Alfie in *Alfie* (2004), a role originated by Michael Cain in *Alfie* (1966), and then starred alongside Michael Caine in 2007's *Sleuth* in a role Michael Caine originated in 1972's *Sleuth*.

◄ Billy and Wyatt (played by Dennis Hopper and Peter Fonda) easily ride **motorcycles** on their trip along the highways.

◄ Jude Law

2002'S **THE HOURS** FEATURES THREE STORYLINES THAT TAKE PLACE IN THREE DIFFERENT DECADES, ONE OF WHICH CENTERS AROUND _____, AN AUTHOR WHOSE WORK INFLUENCES THE WOMEN IN THE OTHER TWO.

▶ Nicole Kidman played **Virginia Woolf**, whose 1925 book *Mrs. Dalloway* influenced author Michael Cunningham's book the movie was based upon. Both follow characters through the course of one day.

AS THE TITLE CHARACTER, _____ DID ALL HIS OWN SINGING IN **RAY**, 2004'S BIOPIC ABOUT RAY CHARLES.

▶ **Jamie Foxx**, an accomplished musical artist in his own right, sang all of Ray Charles' hits in the film, and won an Oscar for it.

POSING AS A FAKE PSYCHIC, ODA MAE BROWN DISCOVERS SHE'S ACTUALLY A REAL ONE WHEN SHE CAN HEAR SAM IN 1990'S _____.

► Whoopi Goldberg won an Oscar for **Ghost**, in which she played Oda Mae, a medium middleman between the deceased Sam, played by Patrick Swayze, and his girlfriend, played by Demi Moore.

IN **SILKWOOD**, TITLE CHARACTER KAREN SILKWOOD, HER ROOMMATE DOLLY, AND BOYFRIEND DREW ALL WORK IN A _____.

► The 1983 film follows Meryl Streep, Cher, and Kurt Russell's characters as they work and uncover corruption in a plutonium-processing plant.

WHAT DISEASE DOES SHELBY SUFFER FROM IN 1989'S **STEEL MAGNOLIAS?**

▶ Though **diabetes** is usually manageable through diet and medication, Shelby defies her doctors and ultimately dies from complications stemming from the stress pregnancy and childbirth has on her diabetic body.

THOUGH INTENDED FOR USE ON ANIMALS, HITMAN ANTON CHIGURH USES A _____ TO KILL PEOPLE.

▶ In *No Country for Old Men*, Joel and Ethan Coen's 2007 adaptation of Cormac McCarthy's novel, Javier Bardem's stone-faced and driven killer's weapon of choice is a **bolt gun.**

ONE OF THE CONS IN 2013'S **AMERICAN HUSTLE** INVOLVES CATCHING POLITICIANS FROM _____ TAKING ILLEGAL BRIBES.

- A NEW YORK
- B NEW JERSEY
- C FLORIDA
- D CALIFORNIA
- E PENNSYLVANIA

▶ Based upon actual events, the film chronicled how many politicians from **New Jersey,** including the well-liked mayor of Camden, played by Jeremy Renner, were caught up in a scheme that would funnel money into their pockets as well as the coffers of Atlantic City.

IN 2012'S **LINCOLN**, DANIEL DAY LEWIS PORTRAYED THE PRESIDENT WHO LOBBIED FOR CONGRESS TO PASS THE _____ AMENDMENT.

▶ **The 13th Amendment,** ratified in 1865, served to codify the principles Lincoln put forth in his 1863 Emancipation Proclamation. It reads in part, "Neither slavery nor involuntary servitude, except as a punishment for crime whereof the party shall have been duly convicted, shall exist within the United States, or any place subject to their jurisdiction."

IN 2008'S MILK, HARVEY MILK, PLAYED BY SEAN PENN, IS ELECTED TO _____, MAKING HIM THE FIRST OPENLY GAY MAN TO BE ELECTED TO PUBLIC OFFICE IN CALIFORNIA.

► Based on true events, Milk was elected to **The San Francisco Board of Supervisors** in 1977. He and San Francisco's mayor, George Moscone (played by Victor Garber), were assassinated by Supervisor Dan White (played by Josh Brolin) in 1978.

BONUS QUESTION

Name the director who portrayed famed director Cecil B. DeMille in *Sunset Boulevard*, a 1950 movie about making movies.

► Cecil B. DeMille (he plays himself)

WHICH COLLEGE DOES "BIG MIKE" OHER, PLAYED BY QUINTON AARON, CHOOSE TO ATTEND IN 2009'S THE BLIND SIDE?

A NOTRE DAME

B THE UNIVERSITY OF MISSISSIPPI

C THE UNIVERSITY OF TENNESSEE

D SYRACUSE UNIVERSITY

E LOUISIANA STATE UNIVERSITY

◀ Oher, like the real football player whose story the film was based on, attended The University of Mississippi, also known as "Ole Miss."

WHO WINS THE FIGHT BETWEEN ROCKY BALBOA AND APOLLO CREED IN ROCKY?

▶ 1976's Best Picture Oscar went to Sylvester Stallone's boxing drama in which **Rocky loses the** fight, but wins the girl of his dreams, Adrian, played by Talia Shire.

WHICH OF THE FOLLOWING UNITED STATES PRESIDENTS IS NOT PORTRAYED IN 2013'S LEE DANIELS'

THE BUTLER:

A DWIGHT D. EISENHOWER

B RICHARD NIXON

C RONALD REAGAN

D BILL CLINTON

E JOHN F. KENNEDY

BONUS QUESTION

Name the legendary actor who starred in only three films: 1955's *Rebel Without a Cause* and *East of Eden*, and 1956's *Giant*.

◄ Though the real-life Cecil Gaines (whose name is actually Eugene Allen), played by Forest Whitaker, worked in the White House for Eisenhower (played by Robin Williams), Nixon (John Cusak), Reagan (Alan Rickman), and Kennedy (James Marsden), he did not work for President Clinton.

◄ James Dean

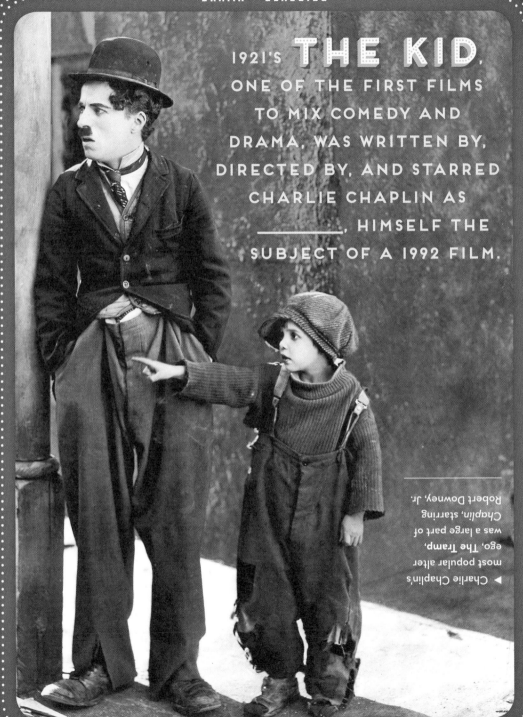

1921'S **THE KID**, ONE OF THE FIRST FILMS TO MIX COMEDY AND DRAMA, WAS WRITTEN BY, DIRECTED BY, AND STARRED CHARLIE CHAPLIN AS _____, HIMSELF THE SUBJECT OF A 1992 FILM.

◀ Charlie Chaplin's most popular alter ego, The Tramp, was a large part of Chaplin, starring Robert Downey, Jr.

BASED ON THE 1936 PLAY BY CLARE BOOTHE LUCE, 1939'S _____ STARRED JOAN CRAWFORD, NORMA SHEARER, ROSALIND RUSSELL, AND NO MEN.

▶ The entire cast of *The Women* was female.

SIDNEY LUMET DIRECTED **12 ANGRY MEN**, A FILM IN WHICH THE TITLE CHARACTERS ARE NEVER NAMED, BUT DESIGNATED IN THE CREDITS BY THEIR PLACEMENT IN A _____.

▶ The 12 characters in the 1957 film, including those portrayed by Henry Fonda, Jack Klugman, Martin Balsam, and E.G. Marshall, comprise a *jury* debating the guilt or innocence of an accused murderer.

2005's WALK THE LINE

tells the story of which country music couple:

A June Carter Cash and Johnny Cash

B Tammy Wynette and George Jones

C Tonya Tucker and Glen Campbell

D Loretta Lynn and Doolittle Lynn

E Patsy Cline and Charlie Dick

► While Sissy Spacek and Tommy Lee Jones played the Lynns in 1980's *Coal Miner's Daughter*, and Jessica Lange and Ed Harris played Patsy Cline and Charlie Dick in 1985's *Sweet Dreams*, it was Reese Witherspoon and Joaquin Phoenix who starred as **June Carter Cash and Johnny Cash** in this film.

IN 1987'S MOONSTRUCK, THE CASTORINI FAMILY LIVE IN _____.

A THE BRONX

B QUEENS

C MANHATTAN

D STATEN ISLAND

E BROOKLYN

◄ Loretta (played by Cher) and her family (including mother, played by Olympia Dukakis, and father, played by Vincent Gardenia) live, work, and love in **Brooklyn**, New York.

One of the first, if not the most popular, feature films to focus on the AIDS epidemic, this award-winning film from 1993 starred Tom Hanks and Denzel Washington as _____.

◄ In Philadelphia, the actors played Andrew Beckett and Joe Miller, lawyers who sue Beckett's employers for wrongful termination.

BONUS QUESTION

Name the actress who starred in *The Amazing Spider-Man* (2012) and *Birdman* (2014).

◄ Emma Stone

1951'S

THE AFRICAN QUEEN

WAS ABOUT A BOAT
CAPTAIN AND A
MISSIONARY SAILING AN
AFRICAN RIVER ON A
BOAT NAMED _____.

◄ In an effort to thwart the German forces at the start of World War 1, Captain Charlie Allnut (Humphrey Bogart) and Rose Sayer (Katherine Hepburn) turn *The African Queen*, a tramp steamer, into a torpedo boat.

SOME OF THE
CHARACTERS IN 1978'S
COMING HOME
WERE COMING HOME
FROM _____.

▶ Luke Martin and Bob Hyde (played by John Voight and Bruce Dern), and others, came home from The Vietnam War.

NAME THE EPIC
1974 FILM, ADAPTED FROM
TWO OF THE HOTTEST NOVELS
PUBLISHED, THAT BURNED
WITH A RARELY-SEEN, ALL-STAR,
MULTI-GENERATIONAL CAST.

▶ Boasting a cast that included (get this lineup) Steve McQueen, Paul Newman, Faye Dunaway, Fred Astaire, Robert Vaughn, Robert Wagner, Richard Chamberlain, William Holden, Jennifer Jones, O.J. Simpson, and more, *The Towering Inferno* was based on *The Tower* by Richard Martin Stern and *The Glass Inferno* by Thomas N. Scortia and Frank M. Robinson.

1940'S

THE GRAPES OF WRATH

CONCERNS THE

JOAD FAMILY

DEALING WITH LOSING THEIR FARM IN THE MIDDLE OF

———————————— •

▶ **The Great Depression,** which was hard on the entire country, especially farmers, was represented in John Steinbeck's 1939 book and on screen by the family portrayed by Henry Fonda, John Carradine, and Jane Darwell, who had to give up their land and search for work—and a home—elsewhere.

Name the actress who fought and loved her husband George in *Who's Afraid of Virginia Woolf?* (1966) and fought and loved Caesar in *Cleopatra* (1963).

▶ Elizabeth Taylor

NAME CHUCK NOLAND'S QUIET, YET FAITHFUL, FRIEND FROM 2000'S

CAST AWAY.

A WILSON

B WILBUR

C WALLY

D WASHINGTON

E WARNER

► Named after the sporting goods manufacturer, volleyball **Wilson** was Chuck's (Tom Hanks) only companion on the island.

DRAMA + CLASSICS

Q True or False: The faceless villain in *The Usual Suspects* is legendary German war criminal Kaiser Schultz.

Q True or False: *Citizen Kane* was the first major motion picture to be filmed entirely in color.

Q True or False: *The Good, the Bad, and the Ugly* is actually the first in a trilogy of films starring Clint Eastwood.

Q True or False: In the classic movie *Casablanca*, none of the characters ever actually set foot in the city of Casablanca.

Q True or False: The famous quote "What we've got here is a failure to communicate" is spoken by the prison warden in *Cool Hand Luke*.

Q True or False: The 1993 western *Tombstone* stars Val Kilmer as Wyatt Earp and Kurt Russell as his longtime friend Doc Holliday.

Q True or False: Among the nicknames handed out by the famous drill sergeant in *Full Metal Jacket* are "Joker," "Cowboy," and "Gomer Pyle."

Q True or False: In 1939's *The Wizard of Oz*, starring Judy Garland, Dorothy's house lands on and kills the Wicked Witch of the East.

Q True or False: While 1974's *Chinatown* is regarded as one of the greatest films ever made, it has a lesser-known sequel called *The Two Jakes*.

A False. The villain manipulating things behind the scenes is criminal mastermind Keyser Soze.

A False. *Citizen Kane* (1941) was filmed in black and white, but even if it had been filmed in color, many other films would have beaten it to the punch.

A False. The film is part of Sergio Leone's *Dollars* trilogy, but it is the final film, not the first.

A False. The film is named for the city in which it takes place.

A True. The line is widely considered to be one of the best in cinema history.

A False. Both actors do star in the film, but Earp is played by Russell and Holliday is played by Kilmer.

A True. The nicknames stick, following many of the characters throughout the film.

A True. The Witch's sister, the Wicked Witch of the West, hounds Dorothy throughout the film, looking for revenge.

A True. *The Two Jakes*, released in 1990, also starred Jack Nicholson, but failed to recoup even half of its budget.

DRAMA + CLASSICS

Q True or False: In *The Shawshank Redemption*, the poster used by Andy (Tim Robbins) to cover up his escape tunnel features Farrah Fawcett in her famous swimsuit.

Q True or False: The Bubba Gump Shrimp Company paid a then-record $2 million for product placement in *Forrest Gump*.

Q True or False: Sean Connery won Best Supporting Oscar at the Academy Awards for his role as Jimmy Malone in 1987's *The Untouchables*.

Q True or False: Kiefer Sutherland, famous for his role as Jack Bauer in television's "24," made his feature film debut in 1992's *A Few Good Men*.

Q True or False: The title of the movie *Rain Man* actually refers to "Raymond" (Dustin Hoffman), the autistic brother of Charlie Babbitt (Tom Cruise).

Q True or False: Dalton Trumbo, the screenwriter of *Spartacus*, was blacklisted by Hollywood for alleged Communist sympathies at the time of the film's release.

Q True or False: *Rebel Without a Cause* was the final film that James Dean would star in before his death.

Q True or False: *Scarface*, which features Al Pacino as mobster and drug lord Tony Montana, was actually a remake of an earlier film.

A False. The poster actually features a scantily clad Raquel Welch.

A False. The Bubba Gump Shrimp Company was a fictional creation of the film, and only later inspired the creation of a restaurant chain bearing that name.

A True. It was in *The Untouchables* that Connery delivered his now-famous "knife to a gunfight" line.

A False. Sutherland does appear in the film, but had been acting for nearly a decade by that time.

A True. The two were separated at a young age, and Charlie falsely remembered Raymond as an imaginary friend named "Rain Man."

A True. Trumbo refused to answer questions about his supposed Communist involvement and was subsequently blacklisted by much of Hollywood.

A False. Although *Rebel Without a Cause* would come to symbolize Dean's life, his final film was *Giant*, released one year later.

A True. The original, less well-known *Scarface* was a 1932 film starring Paul Muni as Tony Camonte.

DRAMA + CLASSICS

Q True or False: *There Will Be Blood* won the Academy Award for Best Picture in 2007, beating out fellow finalist *No Country for Old Men.*

Q True or False: Mel Gibson both acted in and directed *Braveheart.*

Q True or False: One of the first roles played by Haley Joel Osment, best known for his performance as Cole in *The Sixth Sense,* was a small part in *Forrest Gump.*

Q True or False: *Lawrence of Arabia* is the longest film to ever win the Academy Award for Best Picture.

Q True or False: The angel assigned to save George (James Stewart) in *It's a Wonderful Life* is named Charles.

Q True or False: 2003's *Lost in Translation* was Sofia Coppola's directorial debut.

Q True or False: The 1976 science fiction classic *Logan's Run* is set in a dystopian society where nobody is allowed to live past the age of 30.

Q True or False: In *The Silence of the Lambs,* Hannibal Lecter (Anthony Hopkins) helps young FBI trainee Clarice Starling (Jodie Foster) identify a serial killer known as the Zodiac Killer.

A False. It was *No Country for Old Men* that beat out *There Will Be Blood* for the award, with the two movies widely considered to be the runaway frontrunners.

A True. Gibson won Best Director at the Academy Awards, and the film itself won Best Picture.

A True. Osment had a small role as Gump's son, Forrest Gump, Jr.

A True. At 222 minutes (during its original release), *Lawrence of Arabia* is about one minute longer than its closest competition, *Gone with the Wind.*

A False. Clarence Odbody, Angel 2nd Class, is given the task of showing George how wonderful life truly is.

A False. The film was Coppola's second directorial effort. She had directed *The Virgin Suicides* four years prior.

A True. Every citizen is implanted with a "life clock," and agents known as "Sandmen" are employed to track down "Runners" who attempt to escape their fate when their time has run out.

A False. While the Zodiac Killer is a frequent source of inspiration for thriller films, the killer in *The Silence of the Lambs* goes by "Buffalo Bill."

ANIMATED

The unmistakable draw of these films invited you
to laugh, cry, and sing along with more anthropomorphized
creatures than a sugar-inspired fever dream!

WHAT DOES
GASTON
USE IN ALL OF HIS
DECORATING?

► The villain of 1991's *Beauty and the Beast* sings about incorporating **antlers** in all of his design choices.

► As played by Meg Ryan, Grand Duchess **Anastasia**, escaped her family's fate at the hands of Rasputin, played by Christopher Lloyd.

NAME THE 1997 MUSICAL BASED ON THE SPECULATED LIFE OF A MISSING RUSSIAN ROYAL.

► Littlefoot, Cera, and their friends are searching for the **Great Valley**, a place as-yet untouched by drought, where they can live happily ever after.

THE DINOSAURS IN 1988'S THE LAND BEFORE TIME ARE JOURNEYING TO WHAT PLACE?

1992'S **FERNGULLY**

IS THE LAST:

- **A** DESERT
- **B** GRASSLAND
- **C** STILLWATER
- **D** CORAL REEF
- **E** RAINFOREST

▶ **Fairies, shrunken men, and animals of various shapes and sizes try to save the last rainforest** from big, bad, and polluty Hexxus.

NAME GRU'S THREE ADOPTED DAUGHTERS IN 2010'S **DESPICABLE ME**.

▶ Though he didn't mean to at first, Gru, voiced by Steve Carrell, can't help but feel paternal for **Margo, Edith, and Agnes** (voiced by Miranda Cosgrove, Dana Gaier, and Elsie Kate Fisher).

BASED ON THE 1978 PICTURE BOOK BY JUDI AND RON BARRETT, THIS 2009 FILM COULD THEORETICALLY BE VIEWED ON BOTH "THE WEATHER CHANNEL" AND "THE COOKING CHANNEL."

◄ Appealing to audiences of all ages (as well as those interested in both gastronomy and meteorology), the creators of the pun-filled *Cloudy with a Chance of Meatballs*, starring Bill Hader and Anna Faris, cooked up a sequel in 2013.

THE CENTRAL CHARACTERS IN 2005'S **MADAGASCAR** START THE FILM AS RESIDENTS OF WHAT WORLD FAMOUS ZOO?

- (A) SAN DIEGO ZOO
- (B) BRONX ZOO
- (C) DISNEY'S ANIMAL KINGDOM
- (D) PHILADELPHIA ZOO
- (E) THE CENTRAL PARK ZOO

◄ Alex the lion, Marty the zebra, Melman the giraffe, and Gloria the hippo hail from New York's Central Park Zoo.

IN 2010'S **TANGLED**, RAPUNZEL FINDS THAT WHEN NOT FRYING UP SOME EGGS, A _____ IS USEFUL IN A FIGHT.

► A princess may need to defend herself or cook something, so it's good to keep a frying pan handy.

NAME LADY TREMAINE'S CAT IN 1950'S **CINDERELLA**.

► While Cinderella's stepmother and stepsisters, Drizella and Anastasia, were abusing her, Lucifer tormented Jaq, Gus, and the other mice.

IN 2011'S **RIO**,
BLU, A _____,
MAKES HIS WAY
TO BRAZIL.

► Blu, voiced by Jesse Eisenberg, is surprised to find other blue macaws, including Jewel, voiced by Anne Hathaway.

BASED ON CHARACTERS
FEATURED ON THE 1960'S
**"THE ROCKY AND
BULLWINKLE SHOW,"**
THIS PAIR OF TIME TRAVELERS
WERE THE STARS OF THEIR
OWN BIG SCREEN MOVIE IN 2014.

► *Mr. Peabody and Sherman*, voiced by Ty Burrell and Max Charles, prove that a dog's best friend is his boy.

IN TIM BURTON'S 1993
THE NIGHTMARE
BEFORE CHRISTMAS
SALLY IS THE CREATION OF
_____, HALLOWEEN TOWN'S
RESIDENT SCIENTIST.

► **Dr. Finkelstein,** voiced by William Hickey, is very fond of his creation, Sally, voiced by Catherine O'Hara, who feels differently and tries (and tries and tries) to escape his control.

ANTAGONIZED BY THE MAIN CHARACTER, FARMERS

BOGGIS, BUNCE, BEAN

AND *BEAN* ARE THE ANTAGONISTS

in _____.

• • • • • • • • • • • • • • •

► In this adaptation of Roald Dahl's 1974 book *Fantastic Mr. Fox*, the farmers are fed up with Mr. Fox's shenanigans.

BONUS QUESTION

This actor/dancer/director was *An American in Paris* in 1951 who went *Singin' in the Rain* in 1952.

► Gene Kelly

127

TWO OF THE GARGOYLES IN 1996'S THE HUNCHBACK OF NOTRE DAME WERE NAMED AFTER _____, THE AUTHOR OF THE ORIGINAL 1831 BOOK.

▶ **Victor Hugo,** who also wrote Les Misérables, was the inspiration for Victor (voiced by Charles Kimbrough) and Hugo (voiced by Jason Alexander). The name of the third gargoyle, Laverne (voiced by Mary Wickes), was added as an homage to The Andrews Sisters, a singing group from the 1950s whose members included Patty, Maxene, and LaVerne Andrews.

BONUS QUESTION

Name the actress who won an Oscar for playing *The Country Girl* (1954) but went on to marry the Prince of Monaco in real life.

◀ Grace Kelly

Name all seven dwarves from 1937's

SNOW WHITE

AND THE SEVEN DWARFS

in alphabetical order.

◄ Bashful, Doc, Dopey, Grumpy, Happy, Sleepy, Sneezy

THE BEATLES
HAD TO FACE WHAT
NOTORIOUS MUSIC-HATING
CREATURES IN 1968'S
YELLOW SUBMARINE

A. RED MEANIES
B. BLUE MEANIES
C. YELLOW-BELLIED COWARDS
D. GREEN-EYED MONSTERS
E. CONGRESS

► John, Paul, George, and Ringo led a musical adventure to protect Pepperville from the **Blue Meanies.**

IN THEIR SELF-TITLED 2003 FILM, THESE OLDER LADIES ARE REMARKABLE MUSICIANS AND AGILE BICYCLISTS.

► *The Triplets of Belleville* may not say much, but they prove their love and devotion to their music and their friend, Champion.

PRINCE CHARMING AND _____, VOICED BY JENNIFER SAUNDERS, SCHEME TO BREAK UP FIONA AND SHREK IN 2004'S **SHREK 2**.

► Audiences may not have wished to see a villainous **Fairy Godmother**, but they sure were surprised.

WHAT IS HUMPTY DUMPTY'S MIDDLE NAME IN 2011'S **PUSS IN BOOTS**?

A ALVIN

B ANDREW

C ALEXANDER

D ALFRED

E ARTHUR

▶ Puss's childhood friend's full name is Humpty **Alexander** Dumpty.

BASED ON THE BEST-SELLING GRAPHIC NOVEL OF THE SAME NAME, _____ TELLS THE STORY OF A YOUNG GIRL GROWING UP IN IRAN IN 1979.

▶ 2007's **Persepolis** tells Marjane Satrapi's story of what it was like to be a girl while the Islamic Revolution raged in Persepolis.

IN 1986'S **AN AMERICAN TAIL**, FIEVEL AND THE OTHER IMMIGRANT MICE ARE UNDER THE IMPRESSION THAT THERE ARE NO _____ IN AMERICA.

▶ Though it is a land of opportunity, the mice are disheartened to learn that there are, indeed, **cats** in America, and the streets are not paved with cheese.

EDNA MODE'S DESIGNS NEVER INCLUDE A _____.

▶ As fashion designer for the heroes in 2004's *The Incredibles*, Edna, voiced by Brad Bird, will never make a costume with a cape.

THIS 1990 ANIMATED SEQUEL TO A 1977 ANIMATED FILM FOUND ITS PROTAGONISTS, BERNARD AND BIANCA, TRAVELING TO ANOTHER CONTINENT.

▶ *The Rescuers Down Under* reunited the Bob Newhart and Eva Gabor-voiced mice on an Australian adventure.

CAROL BURNETT PROVIDES THE VOICE OF A KANGAROO IN WHICH DR. SEUSS ADAPTATION?

A HOW THE GRINCH STOLE CHRISTMAS
B THE LORAX
C HORTON HEARS A WHO!
D THE CAT IN THE HAT
E GO, DOG, GO!

▶ Many animals, including Kangaroo, don't believe that *Horton Hears a Who!*

WHAT IS "NIMH" AN ACRONYM FOR in THE SECRET OF NIMH?

► In the 1982 film, NIMH (or the National Institute of Mental Health) had experimented on rats and mice, giving them superior intelligence. Based on Robert C. O'Brien's "Mrs. Frisby and the Rats of NIMH," it was the first feature film directed by Don Bluth, who would go on to produce and direct such films as 1986's An American Tail and 1989's All Dogs Go to Heaven.

135

ANIMATED

Q In *The Iron Giant*, the Giant (Vin Diesel) is inspired by superhero comics depicting Batman saving the world.

Q True or False: The Disney movie *Aladdin* takes place in the Kingdom of Arabia.

Q True or False: The letters "A.E." in the title of animated science fiction adventure *Titan A.E.* stand for "After Earth."

Q True or False: The WALL-E's full designation in Pixar's *WALL-E* is Waste Allocation Load Lifter: Earth Class.

Q True or False: Animated family comedy *Happy Feet* is about a penguin named Mumble, who is unable to sing, but can tap dance.

Q True or False: In *Toy Story 2*, the toys are shocked to learn that Buzz Lightyear (Tim Allen) is actually a rare collector's item worth thousands of dollars.

Q True or False: Brad Bird, who directed Pixar's *The Incredibles*, also directed *The Iron Giant*.

Q True of False: Despite being re-released multiple times over the years, Disney's *Fantasia* was originally released all the way back in 1940.

Q True or False: The plot of *Frozen* is loosely based on *The Snow Queen*, a popular fairy tale created by Hans Christian Andersen.

A False. While the Giant does take an interest in superhero comics, Superman is the character from which he draws inspiration.

A False. The film is set in the fictional land of Agrabah.

A True. The A.E. stands for After Earth, while the Titan is the ship that can save humanity following Earth's destruction.

A True. His companion EVE's name stands for Extraterrestrial Vegetation Evaluator.

A True. Mumble was accidentally dropped when he was still in his egg, rendering him unable to sing.

A False. It is actually Woody who is discovered to be a rare toy, which leads to his theft.

A True. While *The Iron Giant* was a box office flop, *The Incredibles* would go on to be a smash hit.

A True. Since then, the film has gone on to inspire both animated and live-action sequels, as well as concerts, video games, and various other forms of media.

A True. Though the plot does not mirror Andersen's story, story elements and characters were inspired by the work.

ANIMATED

Q True or False: *Cars* was the first Pixar film to not feature a single human character.

Q True or False: The acorn-loving squirrel who has been a fixture of the *Ice Age* franchise is named "Scrat."

Q True or False: The lovable, inflatable hero of *Big Hero 6* was named Betamax, after the old video cassettes.

Q True or False: In *Monsters, Inc.*, the fictional city of Monstropolis is powered by nightmares.

Q True or False: Po, the main character in *Kung Fu Panda*, is voiced by curmudgeonly comedian Lewis Black.

Q True or False: In *Bambi*, Bambi's cheerful rabbit friend is known as "Thumper."

Q True or False: Pixar's *A Bug's Life* was released less than two months after the similarly-themed *Antz*.

Q True or False: The voice of Shrek was originally intended to be legendary comedic actor Chris Farley.

Q True or False: In *Tarzan*, after Tarzan's parents are killed, he is raised by a gorilla named Kala as her own child.

A False. *Cars* does lack humans, but *A Bug's Life* was the first Pixar project to go without any human characters.

A True. Scrat is also featured in several short films of his own.

A False. The character's name is Baymax and bears no relation to the old video cassettes.

A False. The city is powered by children's screams and enlists "scarers" to enter children's rooms through their closet doors and scare them.

A False. Po is voiced not by Lewis Black, but by Jack Black.

A True. So named for his penchant for thumping his foot on the ground, Thumper was voiced by Peter Behn, who was just four years old at the time.

A True. Neither studio was very happy with the other, and a race ensued to see who could release their film first.

A True. Unfortunately, Farley passed away before he could finish recording his dialogue.

A True. Tarzan (Tony Goldwyn) is raised in a troop of gorillas, though he has some difficulty earning their respect.

ANIMATED

Q True or False: In *Wreck-It Ralph*, Ralph (John C. Reilly) is the villainous star of a destruction-based game called "Wreck-It Ralph."

Q True or False: *The Emperor's New Groove* focuses on an unpopular emperor who is accidentally turned into a camel during a botched assassination attempt.

Q True or False: In Disney's *Mulan*, Mulan's speaking voice and singing voice are provided by two separate voice actors.

Q True or False: The mantra "hakuna matata," frequently expressed by Timon and Pumba in *The Lion King*, actually translates to "no worries" in Swahili.

Q True or False: In *The Fox and the Hound*, the bitter and angry Widow Tweed threatens to kill her neighbor's hound if it trespasses on her property.

Q True or False: The five NBA players whose talents are stolen in *Space Jam* are Charles Barkley, Patrick Ewing, Shawn Bradley, Larry Johnson, and Muggsy Bogues.

Q True or False: Kurt Russell, James Spader, and Glenn Close all provided voices for characters in 1987's *The Brave Little Toaster*.

A False. Ralph is definitely the villain, but the game is named after its protagonist, Fix-It Felix, Jr. (Jack McBrayer).

A False. Emperor Kuzco (David Spade) is turned into an animal, but it is a llama rather than a camel.

A True. Ming-Na Wen provides Mulan's speaking voice, while Lea Salonga takes on the role when singing becomes necessary.

A True. The phrase is not unique to the boisterous animal duo.

A False. Widow Tweed is sweet and loving, and it is her aggressive neighbor who threatens to kill her pet fox if he sees it on his property.

A True. The movie also features retired NBA legend Larry Bird in a supporting role, though his talent is not stolen.

A False. The voice cast was not without significant talent, though, and featured the voices of Jon Lovitz, Phil Hartman, and Thurl Ravenscroft (better known as the voice of Tony the Tiger and the singer of "You're a Mean One, Mr. Grinch" from *How the Grinch Stole Christmas*).

BONUS ROUND

EASY

Q True or False: In *Star Wars*, many rebel pilots fly X-Wings, spacecrafts named for the distinctive shape of their wings during flight.

Q True or False: In *E.T. the Extra-Terrestrial*, E.T. is lured out of hiding using a trail of M&M candies.

Q True or False: The classic action drama *Top Gun* is about a squadron of fighter pilots during World War II.

Q True or False: In *Harry Potter and the Sorcerer's Stone*, Harry (Daniel Radcliffe) first meets Hermione Granger (Emma Watson) on the train to Hogwarts.

Q True or False: 1987's *RoboCop* is set in a futuristic, dystopian version of Detroit, Michigan.

Q True or False: The movie *Miracle* is about the United States' Olympic hockey team's unexpected victory over Finland in the 1980 gold medal game.

Q True or False: In Mel Brooks' classic space comedy *Spaceballs*, Brooks plays the President of Planet Spaceball, which is running out of water.

Q True or False: Leonardo DiCaprio won the Academy Award for Best Actor for his portrayal of Jordan Belfort in *The Wolf of Wall Street*.

Q True or False: Judd Apatow's *Superbad* is about a pair of college students celebrating one last party before entering the real world.

A True. When in attack position, an X-Wing's wings form an X.

A False. The trail of candy is actually Reese's Pieces. In fact, Mars, the company that makes M&M's, refused to allow them to be used in the film.

A False. The film takes place during the Cold War era.

A True. It is on the train that he becomes acquainted with Ron Weasley (Rupert Grint), as well.

A True. Crime has overrun much of the city, leading its leaders to take drastic measures.

A False. Although the US did defeat Finland in the gold medal game, *Miracle* is about the US team's victory over the Soviet team in the semifinals, commonly referred to as the "Miracle on Ice."

A False. Planet Spaceball is running out of air, prompting Brooks' character to attempt to steal the air from a neighboring planet.

A False. DiCaprio was nominated for the award, but it went instead to Matthew McConaughey.

A False. The pair (played by Jonah Hill and Michael Cera) are high school students preparing to enter college.

EASY

Q True or False: In *Tommy Boy*, portly protagonist Tommy Callahan III is played by *Saturday Night Live* alum John Candy.

Q True or False: Adam Sandler's sports comedy *The Waterboy* is about a misfit waterboy who becomes an unstoppable baseball player.

Q True or False: In 1989's *Major League*, Charlie Sheen's character is nicknamed "Wild Thing."

Q True or False: In *Bruce Almighty*, Jim Carrey's character, Bruce Nolan, is a field reporter for a local television station.

Q True or False: The movie *Ocean's Eleven* takes its title from the name of George Clooney's character in the film.

Q True or False: In *The Prestige*, the part of Nikola Tesla is played by glam rocker David Bowie.

Q True or False: The popular romantic comedy *10 Things I Hate About You* is loosely based on Shakespeare's famous play, *Romeo and Juliet*.

Q True or False: In Quentin Tarantino's *Reservoir Dogs*, John Travolta and Samuel L. Jackson play a pair of cheeseburger-loving hitmen.

Q True or False: The assassination attempt central to the plot of *Inglourious Basterds* takes place at a Parisian hotel.

A False. The titular Tommy is played by fellow *SNL* alum Chris Farley.

A False. In *The Waterboy*, Sandler's character becomes an incredible linebacker for a local college football team.

A True. Sheen plays Ricky "Wild Thing" Vaughn, a pitcher with a history of wild pitches, earning him the derisive nickname.

A True. Bruce's dream is to be an anchorman, but he is stymied at every turn by fellow newsman Evan Baxter (Steve Carell).

A True. Clooney plays Danny Ocean, the leader of a crew of con men.

A True. Bowie did have previous acting experience, having made cameos in a number of different film and television projects, and even starring in the film *Labyrinth*.

A False. The movie is based on a Shakespearean play, but that play is *The Taming of the Shrew*.

A False. The characters are from another Tarantino film, *Pulp Fiction*.

A False. The attempt on Hitler's life takes place in a movie theater operated by Shosanna Dreyfus (Mélanie Laurent).

MEDIUM

Q True or False: Daniel Day-Lewis won his first Academy Award for Best Actor for his role as "Bill the Butcher" in 2002's *Gangs of New York*.

Q True or False: In the *Demolition Man* universe, criminals are cryogenically frozen as a form of punishment and rehabilitation.

Q True or False: The 1993 film *The Fugitive*, starring Harrison Ford, was based on a television show from the 1960's.

Q True or False: In romantic comedy *Summer Catch*, Freddie Prinze, Jr. plays a hot baseball prospect playing in Massachusetts' Cape Cod Baseball League.

Q True or False: In *Point Break*, the bank robbers wear masks depicting the faces of former Presidents Washington, Jefferson, Lincoln, and Kennedy.

Q True or False: *The Birdcage*, starring Robin Williams, takes its name from a nightclub owned by Williams' character.

Q True or False: *Con Air*, the 1997 film about the hijacking of a prison aircraft, stars Sean Connery as Cameron Poe, an imprisoned former Army Ranger, who helps resolve the situation.

Q True or False: The 1989 film *National Lampoon's Christmas Vacation* marked the directorial debut for lead actor Chevy Chase.

A False. Day-Lewis first won the award 13 years earlier, for his performance as Christy Brown in 1989's *My Left Foot*.

A True. Sylvester Stallone's character John Spartan is taught how to knit as part of this reeducation program.

A True. The original series run lasted 4 seasons and 120 episodes.

A True. The Cape Cod Baseball League is a real summer league for college baseball players.

A False. Though the robbers do wear the faces of ex-Presidents, the masks depict Presidents Reagan, Carter, Nixon, and Johnson.

A True. The club is owned by Williams' character, while Nathan Lane's character is the establishment's star attraction.

A False. Nicolas Cage, not Connery, stars as Poe.

A False. Not only did Jeremiah Chechik direct the film, but Chevy Chase has never worked as a director.

MEDIUM

Q True or False: In *Catch Me If You Can*, the father of Frank Abagnale (Leonardo DiCaprio) is played by Christopher Walken.

Q True or False: In Christopher Nolan's *Interstellar*, the black hole around which the potentially habitable planets orbit is known as Giganta.

Q True or False: In *Stripes*, the top secret military project stolen by Privates Winger (Bill Murray) and Ziskey (Harold Ramis) is an assault vehicle designed to look like a mobile home.

Q True or False: *Good Will Hunting* was Minnie Driver's film debut.

Q True or False: 1982's *Rambo* is the first film in which Sylvester Stallone's John Rambo character appears.

Q True or False: The famous line "Greed, for lack of a better word, is good," comes from Martin Scorsese's film *Casino*.

Q True or False: The spaceship in *Pitch Black* crash-lands on a deserted planet after passing through a comet tail and sustaining damage from the debris.

A True. Walken plays the role of Frank, Sr., the indebted patriarch of the Abagnale family.

A False. The black hole's name is Gargantua.

A True. The pair steal the EM-50 Urban Assault Vehicle and use it to sneak into West Germany to visit their girlfriends.

A False. Driver had appeared in six previous films, including the Bond movie *GoldenEye*.

A False. The first film in the Rambo saga was titled *First Blood*. *Rambo*, the fourth film in the series, came out in 2008.

A False. It was Michael Douglas who delivered the line as Gordon Gekko in 1987's *Wall Street*.

A True. The debris disables the ship and thrusts the crew into a fight for their lives.

HARD

Q True or False: Terry Gilliam, the director of such films as *Brazil, Fear and Loathing in Las Vegas*, and *12 Monkeys*, was a member of famous British comedy troupe Monty Python.

Q True or False: Each of Wes Anderson's first three films (*Bottle Rocket, Rushmore,* and *The Royal Tenenbaums*) was co-written with actor Owen Wilson.

Q True or False: Johnny Depp plays famous gonzo journalist Hunter S. Thompson in cult classic *Fear and Loathing in Las Vegas*.

Q True or False: The first feature-length film directed by Christopher Nolan (*The Dark Knight, Interstellar*) was 2000's *Memento*.

Q True or False: The movie *Gattaca* ends with Al Pacino's character repeatedly screaming Gattaca! Gattaca! Gattaca!

Q True or False: The crew of criminals led by Neil McCauley (Robert De Niro) in *Heat* includes characters played by Val Kilmer, Tom Sizemore, and Danny Trejo.

Q True or False: In the movie *Serpico*, Frank Serpico (Al Pacino) plays a corrupt cop facing exposure for his many crimes.

Q True or False: In *Idiocracy*, Joe (Luke Wilson) and Rita (Maya Rudolph) awaken 5,000 years in the future, after the hibernation experiment in which they are taking part is forgotten.

A True. You may recognize Gilliam from his role as King Arthur's trusty companion Patsy in *Monty Python and the Holy Grail*.

A True. Although he has not co-written any additional films with Anderson, Wilson has been involved with many subsequent Anderson projects.

A False. Although the character is based on Hunter S. Thompson, his name (in both the film and the book on which it is based) is Raoul Duke.

A True. Although Nolan had directed a pair of short films (*Doodlebug* and *Following*), *Memento* was his first feature-length effort.

A False. Al Pacino does not appear in Gattaca, but you may be thinking of his character's cries of Attaca! Attaca! Attaca! in *Dog Day Afternoon*.

A True. Danny Trejo's character is even named after him.

A False. Frank Serpico is the lone good cop in a den of vipers, and works to expose the corruption of his colleagues at great risk to himself.

A False. Horrifying as it sounds, the dystopian future in *Idiocracy* is portrayed as a mere 500 years in the future.

HARD

Q True or False: The movie *The Running Man* is named after a game show in the film's universe.

Q True or False: In *Casino*, Robert De Niro plays an operative for the New York mafia sent to Las Vegas to run a casino on behalf of his bosses.

Q True or False: In *Rounders*, Mike McDermott (Matt Damon) finds himself indebted to a Russian mobster with the nickname "KGB."

Q True or False: The young freedom fighters in 1984's *Red Dawn* name themselves the "Wolverines," after their high school mascot.

Q True or False: In the dark comedy *In Bruges*, Colin Farrell plays a hitman whose boss wants him dead as punishment for accidentally killing a priest.

Q True or False: In the crime film *Se7en*, Detectives Somerset (Morgan Freeman) and Mills (Brad Pitt) hunt a serial killer whose crimes each mimic one of the Biblical seven days of creation.

Q True or False: The distinctive opening credits sequence in 2005's *Lord of War* depicts the life of a bullet, from its creation in a factory to being fired from a gun.

A True. Arnold Schwarzenegger plays an unwilling participant in the gladiatorial-style combat show.

A False. De Niro's character is a player in the Chicago Outfit, not the New York mafia.

A True. In the film, Teddy KGB, played by John Malkovich, is a legendary player in underground gambling circles.

A True. The Wolverines fight back to free America after a Soviet invasion.

A False. The young hitman's previous assignment was actually to kill the priest, but he accidentally killed a small child in the process.

A False. Each of the killer's crimes represents one of the seven deadly sins.

A True. The Buffalo Springfield song "For What It's Worth" plays in the background during the sequence.

COMPLETE THE QUOTE!

1 *The Wizard of Oz:* There's no place like _____.
- A. Kansas
- B. Oz
- C. home
- D. Brooklyn
- E. Paris in the Springtime

2 *The Godfather:* Leave the gun. Take the _____.
- A. car
- B. cat
- C. cannelloni
- D. cannoli
- E. candlestick

3 *Toy Story:* To _____ and beyond!
- A. infinity
- B. Albuquerque
- C. insanity
- D. the toy store
- E. the end of the street

4 *A League of Their Own:* There's no _____ in baseball!
- A. sighing
- B. crying
- C. dying
- D. lying
- E. frying

5 *Dirty Dancing:* I carried a _____.
- A. apple pie
- B. baby
- C. backpack
- D. watermelon
- E. monkey on my back

6 *The Princess Bride:* You rush a miracle man you get _____.
- A. bad advice
- B. a broken heart
- C. lousy sandwiches
- D. rotten miracles
- E. a divorce

7 *Mean Girls:* On Wednesdays we _____.
- A. wait here
- B. wear pink
- C. wander around
- E. wish for a miracle
- F. walk to school

8 *The Lego Movie:* Everything is _____!
- A. Terrible
- B. Status quo
- C. Super
- D. Ruined
- E. Awesome

9 *The Social Network:* Drop the "The." Just "_____." It's cleaner.
- A. Google
- B. Mac
- C. Facebook
- D. Ello
- E. MySpace

10 *A Christmas Story:* You'll shoot your _____.
- A. eye out
- B. cat in the face
- C. bird out of the tree
- D. nose off
- E. foot through your shoe

1 C. home 2 D. cannoli 3 A. infinity 4 B. crying 5 D. watermelon 6 D. rotten miracles 7 B. wear pink 8 E. Awesome 9 C. Facebook 10 A. eye out

11 *The Ten Commandments:* So let it be written. So let it _____.
  A. be read
  B. be done
  C. be remembered
  D. be said
  E. be announced

12 *Brokeback Mountain:* I wish I knew how to quit _____.
  A. my job
  B. binge watching
  C. you
  D. smoking
  E. gaming

13 *Schindler's List:* The list is _____.
  A. on the counter
  B. the answer
  C. the key
  D. death
  E. life

14 *The Dark Knight:* Why so _____?
  A. batty
  B. serious
  C. jokey
  D. two-faced
  E. insane

15 *The Lord of the Rings: The Fellowship of The Ring:* One does not simply _____ into Mordor.
  A. wander
  B. whistle
  C. fly
  D. walk
  E. march

16 *Jerry Maguire:* You had me at _____.
  A. wassup
  B. hello
  C. good morning
  D. howdy
  E. hi

17 *Dreamgirls:* And I am telling you I'm _____.
  A. not going
  B. still singing
  C. stopping dancing
  D. really quitting
  E. still eating

18 *Auntie Mame:* Life's a _____ and most poor suckers are starving to death.
  A. party
  B. buffet
  C. cocktail hour
  D. banquet
  E. sit down dinner

19 *Love Story:* Love means never having to say _____.
  A. you'll be late for dinner
  B. you're sorry
  C. your husband's boring
  D. you're working late again
  E. your wife's too busy

20 *The Hunger Games:* May the _____ in your favor.
  A. odds be ever
  B. stars always shine
  C. cards land in
  D. judges rule in
  E. fates be kind

11 B. be done 12 C. you 13 E. life 14 B. serious 15 D. walk 16 B. hello 17 A. not going 18 D. banquet 19 B. you're sorry 20 A. odds be ever

21 *Fight Club:* The first rule of Fight Club is: _____.

   A. you do not tell the cops about Fight Club

   B. you do not talk about Fight Club

   C. you do not write about Fight Club

   D. you do not bring friends to Fight Club

   E. you do not cry at Fight Club

22 *The Little Mermaid:* Life's full of _____, innit?

   A. salty fish

   B. crashing waves

   C. smooth sailing

   D. tough choices

   E. wicked witches

23 *Star Trek 2: The Wrath of Khan:* I have been, and always shall be, _____.

   A. your friend

   B. your enemy

   C. your second in command

   D. your father

   E. your brother

24 *Love, Actually:* To me, you _____.

   A. are everything

   B. are perfect

   C. are lovely

   D. are beautiful

   E. are the best

25 *The Terminator:* Come with me if _____.

   A. you want to get ice cream

   B. you want to survive

   C. you want to get out of here

   D. you want to live

   E. you want to get your son

21 B. you do not talk about Fight Club   22 D. tough choices   23 A. your friend   24 B. are perfect   25 D. you want to live

INDEX

INDEX

INDEX

ABOUT THE AUTHOR

ROBB PEARLMAN

is the author of *Fun with Kirk and Spock*, *The Wit and Wisdom of Star Trek*, and *I Left You a Present*. Though he can neither add nor subtract without using his fingers, he can tell you the name of the actor in that movie about the guy who was looking for that thing.

ABOUT CIDER MILL PRESS BOOK PUBLISHERS

Good ideas ripen with time. From seed to harvest, Cider Mill Press brings fine reading, information, and entertainment together between the covers of its creatively crafted books. Our Cider Mill bears fruit twice a year, publishing a new crop of titles each spring and fall.

CIDER MILL
PRESS

BOOK
PUBLISHERS

"Where Good Books Are Ready for Press"

Visit us on the Web at
www.cidermillpress.com

or write to us at
PO Box 454
Kennebunkport, Maine 04046